The Rest of the Deer
An Intuitive Study of Intuition

by
Margaret Blanchard

Illustrations by Sowbel

Portland   Maine

Astarte Shell Press, Inc.
P.O. Box 10453
Portland, Maine 04104

Copyright ©1993 by Margaret Blanchard
All rights reserved

No part of this book may be used or reproduced without written permission except in the case of brief quotations embodied in critical articles and reviews.

Library of Congress Cataloguing-in-Publication Data
Blanchard, Margaret, 1938-
    The rest of the deer : an intuitive study of intuition / Margaret Blanchard : illustrations by Sowbel.
       p. cm.
    Includes bibliographical references and index.
    ISBN 0-9624626-7-5 : $14.95
    1. Intuition (Psychology) 2. Women — Psychology. I. Title.
BF315.5.B53   1993
128' .3–dc20   93-23350
                                                                              CIP

Illustrations, including cover: Sowbel, Fort Ann, NY
Book design: Sylvia Sims, Portland, ME
Typesetting: Sally L. Brophy, Cumberland, ME
Printing: McNaughton & Gunn, Saline, MI

1st Printing, 1993

10 9 8 7 6 5 4 3 2 1

ACKNOWLEDGEMENTS

I wish to thank the following people for their help in producing this book:

Mom and Dad, Grandmother and Pop, Bob, Ann and Mary for creating the matrix and community (Josie, John, Mary, Rob) in which my intuitive self could grow;

Sowbel, Bernice and Ann for building with me the context and community in which my intuitive self now flourishes and out of which this book took shape;

Elliot and Rachel for providing shelter and support during the whole process;

Margaret Patrice Slattery, Walter J. Ong, Anne Mulkeen Marcus and Maria Courie for guiding me along the path which led to this study;

Elizabeth Minnich for guiding me through the forest of this study and for helping me see both the forest and the trees;

Pamela DiPesa, Ginny Holmes, Joan Pierroti and Jan Wilkotz for companionship, encouragement, advice and response along the way;

Roni Natov, Judith Arcana and Beatrice Mennis for valuable feedback;

Sowbel for editorial and artistic assistance *par excellence*.

The children, Julia, Jeannie, Laura and Ingrid; Joey, Forest and Roger, who brought such delight and enlightenment to my life during this study; and the children who led me to this study, Robert, Catherine, Patrick and Marguerite, Teddy and Kathy, Mattie and Aaron, Peter and Annie, Corey, Daniel and Jonathan, Ryan and Debbie, Kate and Adam, Diep and Nyjep, Aaron.

My students, who have shared so much and taught me so much;

My friends, who have knowingly and unknowingly provided help: Inez, Jackie, Ellen, Dottie, Audrey, Mardie, JoAnn, Jerry, Tania, Melanie, Pat, Kay, Mary Ann, Dee, Jean, Jackie, Janet, Sylvia, Sarah, Amanda, Joyce, Toby, Pat, Vicki, Nita, Margaret, Bob, Ab, Mary, Suzanne, Bob, Linda, Ed, Jean, Jim, Shirley, Irene, Angela, Moises, Sheila, Harriette, Elizabeth, Rachel, Gail, Rochelle, Mary, Jerry, Sue, Chris, Verbena, Clara, Joyce, Terry; the women of the Grail, of the Growth Center, of *Women*; and my friends in Baltimore, New York, Vermont and Texas.

To Eleanor Haney, Sylvia Sims, Sapphire of Astarte Shell Press for help with the final polishing.

TABLE OF CONTENTS

Introduction 1

Part One: Intuition as a Whole
Chapter One: Intuitive Process 10
Chapter Two: What is Intuition? 30

Part Two: The Process in Depth
Intuitive Experience: Introduction 48
    Chapter Three: One Woman's Intuition 49
    Chapter Four: Intuition Shared 60
Intuitive Language: Introduction 70
    Chapter Five: The Heart Gang 72
    Chapter Six: Symbolic Transformation 90
    Chapter Seven: Learning Intuition 107
Intuitive Action: Introduction 126
    Chapter Eight: Building a House 130
    Chapter Nine: Creating Communities 145
    Chapter Ten: Wider Applications 160

Part Three: Theories about Intuition
    Chapter Eleven: What is "Women's Intuition"? 176
    Chapter Twelve: Mapping Some Distinctions 188

References 201
Index 209

Introduction

WHEN I was three or four, driving across the country with my family, we stopped to eat lunch in a Texas restaurant decorated with a genuine deer head. The dark eyes and soft ears of the deer immediately captured my attention. While everyone else was busy reading menus or playing with salt and pepper shakers, I disappeared. My grandfather found me in the alley next to the restaurant. Puzzled he asked me what I was doing out there.

"Looking for the rest of the deer."

What enabled me to see the whole deer when only part of it showed, I realize now, was intuition.

This book explores, from a variety of perspectives and with a variety of voices, the experience and transformative power of intuition, a realization of wholeness which is simultaneously internal and external. Adding my voice(s) to the complex and varied conversation about intuition which has been going on for centuries, I focus on the process of intuition: entering an experience; viewing it, as if it were the interior of a globe, from all sides; understanding the vitality which illumines it; expressing that energy symbolically; and allowing that symbol to tell its own story.

The actual event of intuition is realizing "everything at once," if only for a moment. Or, as Blake puts it, seeing "the world in a grain of sand, eternity in an hour." Buddha used intuitive language when, instead of giving a verbal sermon, he held up a flower to his disciples. Only one of them, in an intuitive flash, received the insight, the realization not only of the life and death of each being, but also an understanding of the Buddhist philosophy about suffering and detachment.

Intuition is nothing new. Neither is the idea, which I explore in this book, of women's intuition. What is unique about this book is that it offers a new perspective, grounded in the theory and practice of the women's movement, with which to view this ancient concept and reality. Combined with insights from depth psychology and from aesthetic theory and practice, this approach allows a new synthesis, one which can enrich each of the separate sources with which it interacts. Each of these different streams meets at the common ground of story telling which is central to intuitive process.

What the women's movement brings to this study of intuition is a heightened awareness of process. This book, as a result, emphasizes the process of intuition which is available to us all rather than the products of intuition whose value, as with many other productions in this culture, is recognized only in a few works of "genius." The women's movement (along with other civil rights and recovery movements) has shown us how empowering the telling of our stories can be. This study of intuition can bring to feminist/womanist practice an understanding of how transformative telling our stories in an intuitive way can be. Just as feminism has given us a new awareness of some of the hidden dimensions of our everyday language, an understanding of intuition can give us a deeper grasp of our own symbolic language. This language can help us express experiences which have been left out of the dominant discourse either because they have been silenced or because they cannot be expressed in ordinary language.

The study of intuition, in turn, gives aesthetic grounding to self-disclosure, which is often, in current usage, considered a therapeutic practice. While various expressive arts therapies bring an awareness of the creative process into their practice, all too often the gap between healing and creativity is never fully bridged. The myth of the true artist requires artists to pay for their creative freedom with isolation, alienation and madness (and then offers reverence when they commit suicide or otherwise drop out.) People who aspire to mental health often spend considerable time and money talking their way into "normality." Those who do choose to explore the fertile ground of creativity between the mainstream of "sanity" and the outposts of art often pay dearly for workshops and weekends to learn something which is easily accessible and could have been nourished for free in their earliest schooling through something as basic as story-telling.

If nothing else, this book can serve to demystify intuition, an experience which is available to anyone who can read this book and to many others who can't. Intuition is not a gift reserved for the artistic, intellectual, or psychic elite; it is a human potential which can be developed in every one of us. While the importance of intuitive (creative, artistic) learning for everyone cannot be emphasized too much, it is never too late to tap into this ability. This book joins others in providing encouragement and skills.

I hope what is written here will also encourage those who have already developed their intuitive abilities to integrate them into their action in the world, personally and politically. There is much talk in some circles these days about "trusting your intuition," but few have the courage to do that, much less acknowledge that they have acted on it.

The uses of intuition are many, not just artistic, not just therapeutic. The view of the whole which intuition offers is essential for envisioning the future and resolving dilemmas in regard to the economy, the environment, national and international disputes. As multicultural issues come into focus, both in the United States and elsewhere, the intuitive faculty which makes connections in the face of diversity will be crucial for social tolerance, respect and appreciation of others.

Out of the particular feminist/womanist perspective I bring to this study and because of the relevance of this study to multicultural issues, I explore throughout this book the theme of intuition and community. As I explain in the first chapter, I believe that buried within the divisive shell of the term *women's intuition* is a process which can help us all negotiate the tension between self and social context. Because intuition allows multiplicity within wholeness, it encourages respect for the uniqueness of each individual person within the whole community and for each cultural identity within the whole society.

The book is divided into three parts. In the first part I look at intuition as a whole, focusing first on the intuitive process and on some descriptions of intuition. I save detailed distinctions between the intuitive, the rational, the psychic and the mystic until the end of the book. While definition is usually a starting place in the discursive mode of thinking, it is often the ending stage of an intuitive process. Intuition usually starts at the center of personal experience and then expands outwards toward definition. If one tries to pin it down too soon, it, like a live butterfly, will flutter away.

The second part of the book goes more deeply into three basic aspects of the intuitive process: experience, language and action. First I explore intuitive experience from a personal perspective and from the perspective of women students. Next, I examine intuitive language in three different contexts: the play of children, the process of women in a college classroom and the work of three women writers. I then look at how intuition translates into action: building a house; building community; and helping to resolve or reframe issues like drug abuse, illiteracy and abortion.

Finally, I return at the end of the book to the theoretical questions I begin with: to the question of women's intuition, the issue of what, if anything, might be "womanly" about intuition as it now exists in women; and to questions about how intuition differs from experiences with which it is often equated: the unconscious, the psychic, the irrational and the mystic.

Each chapter of this book reflects and gains luminosity from the other chapters. As intuition allows us multiplicity within wholeness, these many facets can contribute to a sense of the whole. One facet may allow us to gaze more deeply into the core of the process. Another may reflect our own image. And another may condense a panorama of earth and sky. But each is meant to provide new information about the whole intuitive process.

This study is by necessity interdisciplinary. Psychology, literature, education and philosophy all contribute to our understanding of intuition. Intuition can cross disciplinary boundaries without blurring distinctions among disciplines. Like the old national highways which move from state to state, the intuitive process winds through varying landscapes; unlike superhighways, which make everything look the same—anywhere, USA. And it functions differently in each area. Like farm country, forest, mesa and mountain, each area—psychology, literature, education and philosophy—offers intuition its own context, its own challenges.

Because the intuitive process varies with each person's individual experience, attention must also be paid to the different contexts within which that process is realized. Is the traveler a lone bicycler? Are the travelers a group of folks in an old jalopy? Are the travelers strangers sharing a tour bus? Each of these chapters explores the movement of intuition within a particular context, a context differing by participant (child, adult student, creative writer, group of friends), as well as by discipline.

Although the intuitive process itself makes its own whole, the significance of each of its stages can be highlighted by the perspectives of both context and participant. The initial stage of integration or reintegration of various parts may be healing (in the sense of making whole) for one person, therapeutic for anyone who feels personally fragmented or traumatized (wounded in or cut off from an integral part of self which has been lost or abused). For such a person this first stage can accomplish not just a realization but a recovery of wholeness. A missing piece, like the heart of a jigsaw puzzle, can provide the complete picture. For another person this same stage may be a prelude to creativity or synthesis, an assembling of images or ideas which suddenly and mysteriously fuse into something quite new. For such a person this synthesis is the key experience while for the next person, a crucial realization might come during the stage which often emerges from that synthesis: a transformation which signals a breakthrough in personal growth or issues forth in a shared social vision and program.

Even persons traveling in the same vehicle (a support group, a class, a writer's group) might have different experiences of the same landscape or the same phase of the journey. Students in my intuition class have had a range of experiences: those who need it find personal healing; some discover a creativity they had not realized before; others use the intuitive process to pass through a crucial stage of growth; and still others discover a more expansive way of processing their perceptions of the larger world. A few pass through all of these dimensions during the course.

Underlying these various dimensions is the assumption that we are inherently whole as individuals (even when we feel fragmented and in need of healing). Also, our own health and growth requires us to realize our connections to expanding dimensions of wholeness. Just as organic life grows from seed to sprout to plant to flower to fruit or transforms from egg to larva to pupa to butterfly, so we are called to move from one dimension to another. Intuition does not privilege any one of these stages but realizes in each, as well as in all, a kind of wholeness.

For one person this realization may take place in an educational context, for another in a therapeutic context and for still another in an artistic context. Each of these contexts will give a different energy and shape to the realization.

In actuality, these dimensions exist simultaneously, for any one person. I can be at the same time a fragmented person with parts of me split off or wounded; a person becoming whole by a natural growth process, cracking out of a shell or shedding a skin as part of my maturing; a creative person realizing a vital connection between myself and what I am creating; a social person feeling my place in a larger context of relationships; a political person moved by insight to action; and a spiritual person intuiting a vast network of connection among human, nature and cosmos. An intuitive realization can occur within and can subsequently transform any one of these dimensions or several at once.

So within the intuitive process, what can be distinguished as education or as therapy or as artistic creation can also overlap. Becoming whole can be a form of healing as well as a form of education. Being led forth or out, or branching out like a river (one meaning of *education* in the Oxford English Dictionary), can be a result of learning as well as of artistic creation. Actualization of a latent or potential whole can be stimulated by the creative process as well as produce a mystical realization. Whether the click occurs between one part of self and another, between internal feeling and external perception, between self and other or between one dimension of the world and another, what is essential to the subsequent realization of wholeness is the intuitive process.

Another reason boundaries of discipline, stage or identity cannot contain all of the intuitive process is that because intuition is realization and not just perception or aesthetic appreciation, intuition allows or involves some kind of change. Whether or not the landscape shifts from desert to woods, the person who starts out on the intuitive journey is not the same person who completes it.

Sometimes this change is simply a shift in consciousness that breaks the ground for more fertile insights later. Sometimes it is a sudden synthesis resolving an irreconcilable conflict, releasing new options. Sometimes it is an expansion of identity, a turn in the road which opens up new vistas. Sometimes it allows a shedding of resistances so that a natural maturing can take place more joyfully. And sometimes it provides such a shimmering vision of possibilities that one is moved to action. Whether these changes are subtle or profound, therefore, intuition is ultimately transformative. It can move us from one field of inquiry to another (from psychology to literature), from one stage to another (contraction to exploration), and from one identity to another ("I am a nurturing person" to "I am a creative person.")

Although I do have a working definition of intuition, I invite readers to explore their own definitions as we move through various perspectives. When these concepts have grown toward their own edges, then distinctions, definitions, theories and other ways of talking about intuition will become clearer. It seems easier to tell one flower from another than to distinguish the plants by their bulbs or seeds.

I am reminded of the cartoon showing two birds sitting on a branch peeking over a birdwatcher's shoulder as he examines his birdwatching book. "What kind of bird did he say we are?" One asks the other in modest curiosity.

Clearly our need to know what intuition is does not hamper our ability to be intuitive. As I discovered teaching the intuition course I describe later, everyone seemed to have her own definition of intuition. But still we were able to share some common ground. That experience of multiplicity within wholeness is key to intuitive realization.

In the spirit of Judy Grahn's common woman and with Adrienne Rich's dream of a common language, I hope to speak in this book to what we have in common without mushing over significant and wonderful differences among us. I would like to translate this knowledge for a wider community. Because I have developed many of the ideas in this book in dialogue with other women, friends, activists within the women's movement, students and colleagues, I trust the relevance of issues of identity, language, community and action which our discussions of intuition have raised. I hope this book will serve as one step toward a broader context for that exchange.

Part One
INTUITION AS A WHOLE

CHAPTER ONE

Intuitive Process

BURIED WITHIN the divisive shell of the term *women's intuition* is, paradoxically, the seed of a process by which we can negotiate the tension between self and community, with the greatest respect for both individual identity and variety.

The term *women's intuition* is unfortunately parallel to the term *black magic*. The not-so-subtle undercurrent of sexism in the one and racism in the other are used to devalue both types of knowing—intuition and magic. The term is used to downgrade insights of women by referring, usually in a derogatory manner, to those hunches people get which often signal some kind of E.S.P. In exploring the meanings of intuition, *Roget's Thesaurus* quotes an anonymous pedant: "The strange instinct that tells a woman she is right whether she is or not." This may be why many people (by some accounts, more men than women) prefer to describe their hunches as "gut reactions" rather than "intuitions."

What I mean by intuition is neither hunch nor gut reaction but realization of wholeness, a kind of insight which simultaneously connects both internal and external ways of knowing, giving us "everything at once," if only for a moment. Wholeness here does not refer to a product of abstract generalization but to an apprehension of the energy, animating spirit or dynamism of an experience. This insight usually finds form in an image or symbol and often plays out its dynamic dimension through a story. Sources for this definition are my study of Susanne Langer, John Dewey, Carl Jung and Piero Ferrucci, but this particular synthesis is of my own making.

Intuition, therefore, is an event, not a perspective, not a belief system, definitely not an ideology. As realization of wholeness (or wholenesses) which is simultaneously internal and external, it is an event which is both experiential and cognitive. As such it represents more than a simple link or current between the internal and external, more than just a perception or a projection.

In the intuitive event, the wholeness or dynamism of our internal experience unites momentarily with the wholeness or energy of the external, giving us an intuitive insight. It is analogous to the channeling of electricity from a flash of lightning into a source of power for a home. The circles in the following illustration symbolize the wholeness in each dimension of the dynamic, and therefore temporal, event of intuition. The dotted lines indicate the transient nature of the event.

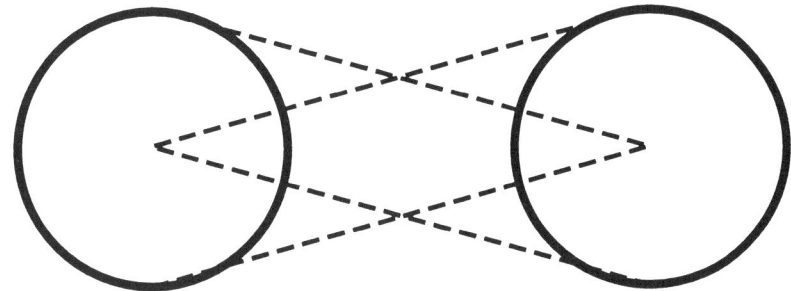

There is no evidence which convinces me that women are inherently more intuitive than men. Actually, there is no way of measuring intuition. Various psychic abilities can be tested (including pre-cognition, knowing what will happen before it happens.) But psychic ability is not the same as intuition. The only instruments available for assessing intuition are personality inventories like the Myers-Briggs, which are essentially self-appraisals and are based on varying definitions of intuition.

Some studies claim that women (and left-handed men) have a larger *corpus callosum*, the network of tissues which connects the hemispheres of the brain. This finding suggests but does not prove a greater integration of the hemispheres of the brain. And that disputed integration may or may not have any connection with intuition which other studies locate in the frontal lobe, where so far no gender differences have been discovered. These findings about gender differences in the structure of the brain are disputed by feminist biologists like Ruth Bleier and Anne Fausto-Sterling, who argue that they are based on insufficient and misleading evidence.

Whatever the scientific interpretations, whatever the biological facts, we do discover, in exploring the gender bias about intuition, that what is called genius in men is very much like what is sometimes called intuition in women—the flash of insight which solves a puzzle, makes a connection, conceives something new.

Such gendered language separates women from men and isolates those, male or female, who are deeply intuitive by making them seem exceptionally foolish or exceptionally wise. Even the term *genius* suggests that only the intellectual elite can experience intuition, whereas intuitive insights are actually available to all of us. Such labeling also undermines one of intuition's most powerful effects, its ability to unify disparate elements.

I won't go into detail at this point about whether, in fact, women are more intuitive than men (I don't believe we are) or whether women, as we are now socialized, have different intuitive perspectives (I believe we do). Instead I want to describe an intuitive process which, perhaps, has been reached more readily by certain creative women who embraced intuition not just because it was assigned to women but also because they affirmed it in themselves. These women have a valuable insider's view of the process, a process which can lead us all toward deeper authenticity and community.

This process is, I believe, at the heart of our ability to drop into our own solitude, affirm both our uniqueness and the uniqueness of others, yet still connect to the communal contexts of other people's stories and our shared heritages of stories. This process is particularly important for women to recognize because of our special issues around the pull to be for others and the need also to be by ourselves. Our lives are sometimes fraught with, sometimes blessed by this tension which is shared, to some extent, with nurturing men.

Only the midpoint of this process is, strictly speaking, *intuition*. Getting in touch with the unifying energy of an experience gives us a realization of wholeness which is simultaneously our own and beyond us. This kind of insight, connecting internal and external ways of knowing, showing everything at once, can, we all know, happen spontaneously, anytime, anyplace. But it does not occur in a vacuum, nor is it static or absolute. Even the most comprehensive intuitions are in process. They grow and change as our insights into ourselves and into the world deepen.

The intuitive process, therefore, while it does not guarantee insight, creates conditions favorable to its sprouting. It also provides a context in which the insight can be expressed. Symbolic expression, in turn, deepens and clarifies the original intuition, setting the stage for further insights. Like the thread which leads the explorer through a labyrinth, this process can clue us to core insights.

Having such insights is not the same as expressing them. Because they give us everything at once, specific intuitions cannot be expressed directly through ordinary speech or discursive language, which is linear, stretched out into parts. They must be symbolic, expressed through the language of art, the symbols of nature, or dream symbolism. This is because symbols allow for simultaneity—the ability to hold disparate and separate components together in one whole long enough for recognition.

The philosopher Susanne Langer explains these two uses of language, both of equal value, as the "discursive" and the "symbolic." In doing so she articulates a key formula: In symbolic language stories follow from images as in discursive language statements follow from words. In symbolic language, the image can expand into narrative, maintaining its wholeness in time, while in discursive language, analysis into parts is held together by generalizing statements (*PNK*, 128).

Nowhere is the need for symbolic language more evident than when we try to describe intuition itself. To express the nature of intuition fully, we must use a symbolic mode of description. Piero Ferrucci calls symbols "the alphabet of the intuition" (225). Among my favorite poetic descriptions of intuition are Emily Dickenson's "a blossom of the brain" (443) and William Blake's "to see the world in a grain of sand, eternity in an hour" (87). Virginia Woolf's phrase, "this wave in the mind," describes intuition: "A sight, an emotion, creates this wave in the mind long before it makes words to fit it"(*AWD*, 152). As does James Joyce's term *epiphany*, for the moment in which "the soul of the commonest object...seems to us radiant" (307).

These metaphors for intuition suggest why Jung speaks of an image "being charged with emotion [whereby] it gains numinosity (or psychic energy) and becomes dynamic [so that] consequences of some kind must flow from it" (*MHS*, 87). Images so charged have become symbols. The consequences include, among other things, the narrative which follows from the image. In other words intuition looks at a seed and sees the wholeness of the particular blossom which will unfold from it as well as the process of that unfolding, its story.

Intuition in Women Writers

Drawing particularly on descriptions by women writers, I'll describe stages of an intuitive process: dropping into unique personal experience, sometimes through empathy or identification with another person or another reality; centering in that experience; viewing it from all sides; getting in touch with the unifying energy of that experience; finding an image to express that dynamism; telling the story which grows out of that image; and allowing that story to expand in meaning and in the context of other stories, including the larger cultural contexts of symbols and myths.

No one understands this process better than those who tell these stories. While there is nothing about their story telling that is fixed or universal—in fact, it is the nature of intuition both to honor the uniqueness of each experience and to welcome multiplicity—these creative processes, such as the following, can be described and shared with others heading down similar trails:

> I learned to make my mind large, as the universe is large, so that there is room for paradoxes (Maxine Hong Kingston, *Woman Warrior*, 34).

> An inner ear is invisible, untouchable, and something lots of folks don't know they have. But that's the ear you hear with when all else fails... And we'll hear all about ourselves if we learn to be quiet and listen (Linda Beatrice Brown, *Rainbow Roun Mah Shoulder*, 136).

> The gift is perhaps not strictly or simply one of foretelling, but is rather the power of seeing (if only for a flash) everything at once: seeing whole (Ursula LeGuin, *The Left Hand of Darkness*, 204).

> It would be necessary to see everything again and again from a dozen different angles before she could begin to understand it (Doris Lessing, *The Marriages Between Zones Three, Four and Five*, 82).

> The best thing we can do is to keep the thought whole in our minds and let it grow (Lessing, 87).

> It is through the unexpected, or the sidelong, or the indirect that truths come our way (Lessing, 140).

> We say a true Flame Bearer has another eye...behind the two

eyes that see the world. This other eye goes right down into the heart. She who sees with this inside eye sees always the meaning in things (Kim Chernin, *The Flame Bearers, 123*).

I am woman with her (though I am man as I write of her femaleness)... I am Ben Ata when I summon him into my mind and try to make him real... Describing we become (Lessing, 198).

Never in my life did I attack such a vague yet elaborate design; whenever I make my mark I have to think of its relation to a dozen others... I am always stopping to consider the whole effect" (Virginia Woolf on *The Waves in a Writer's Diary*, 143).

One of the fullest descriptions of the intuitive dimensions of the creative process is Woolf's account in her diary of the writing of *The Waves*. Beginning in 1926, during one of her depressions, she uses the image of a fin in the water, an image she senses is "the impulse behind another book." In her diary she then follows the evolution of the novel, which she sees as "the idea of some continuous stream... all flowing together."

Calling the incipient book at first *The Moths*, she switches from the central imagery of candle and moths because moths don't fly by day. There can't be a lighted candle for the daytime scenes but the progression from light to dark is essential to the novel's plot. In making this change, she moves from an essentially dualistic structural symbol (the one candle and the many moths are two different realities) to a symbol of water in which the one (ocean) and the many (waves) are from the same element.

Time and again she invokes intuition as the source of her creativity:

But it needs ripening... I should like to take the globe in my hands and feel it quietly, round, smooth, heavy.... I will go backwards and forwards... I am going to let myself down into my mind.... I am always stopping to consider the whole effect.... I press to my centre. I set my hands on something central... But how to pull it together, how to...press it into one.... I believe these illnesses are in my case...partly mystical. Something happens in my mind. It refuses to go on registering impressions. It shuts itself up. It becomes chrysalis.... To do nothing is often my most profitable way.... It will bear expansion. It is compressed, I think.... Then back again to this hideous shaping and molding... Yes, it was the greatest stretch of mind I ever knew... It's done; and, as I certainly felt at the end, not merely finished, but rounded off, completed, the thing stated.... I have netted that fin in the waste of water which appeared to me over the marshes out of my window.... What interests me in the last stage was the freedom and boldness with which my imagination picked up, used and tossed aside all the images, symbols which I had prepared (*AWD*, 101-169).

At the end, in 1932, she refers to "this ecstatic book."

By drawing from these descriptions, as well as the actual practice of Virginia Woolf and the other writers quoted above, I can summarize, to some extent, an intuitive process. It's not *THE* intuitive process since I doubt there is one process that would fit the myriad of ways people intuit, but it is one which touches on most of the possibilities inherent in the process of intuition.

In capsule form: intuition not only adds parts/aspects/ moments together, it integrates them. From that process, it continues to synthesize them, to create something new. And that creation transforms not only that which it brings together, but the person doing the synthesizing—and, potentially, others.

Phases of the Intuitive Process

Let's look more closely now at the various phases of this process. It is helpful to start with an open mind. It wouldn't hurt to have engraved over the portal of the third eye, or wherever intuition resides, the Buddhist saying, "Cease to Have Opinions." In my experience the biggest obstacle to intuitive knowing is too-heavy reliance on preconceived notions and prejudices, on what Buddhists call the judging and comparing mind, or on what some call rationality.

Next, one must be willing to drop into unique, individual experience. This entering into the particular confirms the feminist insistence upon the importance of the personal as a starting point. We do not stand outside, we enter into. Going IN-TO-IT is key to Intuition.

This knowing from within contrasts with abstract generalization which tends to rise above, outside things so that single entities blur into a class or category or idea. This is often called objective knowing in contrast to subjective knowing. Intuition, however, is not just subjective. Intuitive realization occurs at that juncture where inner knowing connects with external awareness. That link is the place of primary integration from which synthesis and transformation can flow.

There are two kinds of experience we can drop into—our own or another's. Being able to drop into our own experience seems to me a prerequisite for dropping into another's. We must be willing to risk knowing from within what Ken Wilbur calls "the real self: the innermost core," quoting both Jesus, "The Kingdom of Heaven is within," and Swami Prabhavananda, "Who, what, do you think you are? Absolutely, basically, fundamentally deep within?" (54).

Once we have dropped into our own experience—and not experience in general but a specific, unique experience—and hope to understand it intuitively, we must center ourselves within that experience. There are various ways of doing this and each person can find those that work best—meditation, being in tune with our body, emotional awareness. We've all experienced what it's like to be uncentered, scattered, maybe anxious, distracted and then the relief that comes when we suddenly drop into the center of our experience, out of physical exhaustion, an emotional outburst or a moment of peace. Without this kind of centering, intuition really has to struggle to be heard. Without this kind of emotional tuning-in, it may not even have a voice.

Once centered, intuition is aided if we're willing to look around, view the situation from all sides. This is somewhat like Jung's method of circumambulating a dream image in order to come to a fuller sense of its meaning.

One wonderful example of this stage of the process can be found in descriptions of *wayfinding*, navigation without instruments 6,000 miles across the Pacific Ocean from Hawaii to Tahiti. Kyselka describes two voyages with different navigators, one trained in the old way and one finding a new way. Although both navigators relied primarily on intuition, one drew on ancient tradition and highly developed sense awareness and the other drew on modern technology and information from astronomy. Reflecting upon the voyage, the younger man observes:

> Navigating without instruments is a personal act. You must know the principles but you cannot reduce wayfinding to a set of formal operations.... When I understand things without knowing why, that's when I know I've taken great steps (206).

The second possible source of intuition is dropping into another's experience, another world, through identification or empathy. This offers itself daily in our work with children, students, clients, our other selves or the world around us. Rather than just knowing about them, we are willing in some sense to become them.

One of my favorite descriptions of this stage of the process comes from the scientific realm—biologist Barbara McClintock's work with corn plants. Not only did she enter that world, she identified with its natives: "I understood every plant."

Commenting on her intimate and total knowledge of the plants, a colleague once remarked that she could write the "autobiography" of each plant she worked with (Keller, 104).

Empathy (feeling with) or identification (being aware of similarities) are preconditions for intuitive insight, facilitating the necessary connection between inside and outside, self and other. But they do not automatically create intuition. In addition to McClintock's intimacy with the plants, she also had an understanding of them. She was not only sharing their feelings and their identity but their experience of life, their actual process and perspective, within the context of a larger process and perspective. There is not just a connection but also an understanding of what that connection means.

This kind of understanding does not result from a simple step-by-step process. While such process analysis is useful here for explaining certain aspects of intuition, it can't possibly describe how intuition actually functions. Intuition neither races toward a goal nor methodically traces its steps. It meanders. And, more importantly, the closer we get to the core of intuitive insight, the more labyrinthine the journey. Rather than progressing forward in a predictable fashion, we stumble over truths, fall into relevant zones, digress into crucial detours. The ultimate insight may arrive in a flash, but we've probably wandered quite a while to get there.

Whenever we drop into another's experience, another world, some fascinating and complex issues arise. There are issues of translation and transformation; of psychic or aesthetic distance; of identity and integrity; of mirroring, exchanging and merging. There is the question of how the transformer becomes transformed in the process of transforming. These are at the heart of feminist discussion of permeable boundaries and are raised in a variety of ways by the women writers I have quoted here.

Speaking of the affection she felt for the pieces that go together, Barbara McClintock noted, "As you look at these things, they become part of you. And you forget yourself" (Keller, 118). Once she was so absorbed in an observation, she forgot her own name. But the self who was involved, the witness self, was still functioning. What self, then, was forgotten? The persona? The ego? How is what Evelyn Fox Keller calls McClintock's "capacity for total absorption" (118) different from co-dependency when transferred to the interpersonal realm?

What is the something that happens in what Elizabeth Minnich calls the in-between ("Translation," 4)? Is it a kind of personal imperialism or a real exchange which transforms both participants? In the psychological realm, Sylvia Perera summarizes the issues of identity and merger between client and therapist. She acknowledges the problems that can arise if the border is too inflexible or too permeable.

Frances Vaughn distinguishes intuitive identification from mere projection and speaks of a balancing "disidentification." This suggests that identification with one part or person, however central or vital, may be key to an intuitive insight, but does not account for the whole of it. Intuition enables us not just to see our own reflection but also to enter into the distinctive energy of another. At the same time, intuition makes connections with larger patterns, larger wholes, not just to connect but also to comprehend.

While, for instance, one may empathize with a disappointed child, intuitively one can extend the process to imagine her disappointment turning into surprise or relief. This insight need not dissolve the intensity of the moment, but it can bring comfort to the comforter. Or we may understand the issue within a wider, more meaningful context: how we respond to hunger will depend on whether it is taking place within a desert during a drought or civil war, or whether it is taking place in a large American city where waste of food is standard operating procedure.

Therapists are called on over and over to employ both empathy and intuition. Were they to empathize or identify with only one member of a family, they might miss understanding her place in the overall pattern of relationships. A really skilled counselor can empathize with each person in a group and, in so doing, balance the tensions through a kind of multifaceted identification and gain insight into the dynamic of the whole.

A particularly dramatic example of such intuitive insight can be found in *The Flock*, an account of multiple personality disorder from the perspectives of both client and therapist. Successful treatment depended on each of them being able to recognize and affirm all of the twenty-four selves inhabiting the same body and to refuse to choose one over another, or as the therapist puts it, "play favorites." The extent of the splitting was communicated intuitively by the client's construction of twenty-four unique snowflakes for the gift of a Christmas tree. This message was intuitively realized by the therapist, Lynn, when the gift was presented to her:

> I counted twenty-four snowflakes on the tree. Isis' message was clear. There were more personalities, each unique and important to the design of the whole (71).

While empathy and identification provide an essential grounding in the particular, intuition juggles these elements within a larger context. In some ways intuition is more like compassion in its spaciousness than it is like empathy. Intuition is an expansiveness of the mind parallel to a compassionate expansion of the heart.

Whether you have dropped into your own experience or some other experience which then becomes, in some sense, your own, for a full intuition, you next will get in touch with the unifying energy, the animating spirit, the dynamism of both self and other which is called forth by this experience. Now you can *realize the whole of the experience*. Here the actual intuition occurs. The process leading up to this point is what makes it possible, but not what causes it. That remains a mystery, along with other events of mind. The intuitive process does not always yield insight. In the same garden, within the same soil, under the same conditions of weather, some seeds germinate and some do not.

Getting in touch with the unifying energy is not so much a reaching out to grasp it as an openness which allows it to touch you. Such receptiveness in our American culture is often considered feminine, another reason intuition is equated with women. Once you receive that vital whole, if you respond with a unifying flame of your own, both participants illuminate each other, for a moment.

This intuitive moment can seem magical, as well as unpredictable and uncontrollable, because it is so charged. It can seem mysterious because it is so ephemeral and so difficult to describe. But it is really no more miraculous than any other kind of human understanding. It carries some of the impact of falling in love, without the grasping or delusion usually characteristic of that state. But it requires a meditative attitude. In order to receive fully the whole energy of the other, one must respond with neither attraction nor aversion but simply acceptance of what's there.

What distinguishes the intuitive moment from some other kind of response or understanding is the vital link between the one knowing and the one known (whether object, environment, animal, person or even another part of self). For a moment the whole of one and the whole of the other connect to provide insight into a unifying, or third, wholeness.

Take for example a view of the whole earth, such as we've been able to see since the first space launches. This perception of wholeness can in itself inspire any number of subjective or emotional responses of discovery or awe, as expressed by many astronauts. It has also led to objective responses which generate such activities as mapping and measuring. None of those responses are in themselves intuitive. But imagine a woman, herself perhaps an astronaut, realizing as she looks at this beautiful globe that the earth is a living, breathing body, vulnerable as her own body to neglect and abuse. In that intuitive moment her wholistic awareness of the earth illumines and is illumined by her wholistic awareness of her body. Out of this intuitive experience a movement such as ecofeminism could have been born. And while this insight reaffirms ancient wisdom, it is for this person entirely fresh.

Because each intuitive moment is a new discovery, it works against, and often destroys, prejudices. What counts is the vital energy of both participants, not their external characteristics. While, of course, people's identities cannot be separated from their energies, any kind of stereotyping makes this intuitive connection impossible.

A friend of mine who does massage describes how she relates to someone's body with her eyes closed and her fingers guiding her to the knots in the muscles and blocks in the energy. As she tells it, all else drops away except what she discovers with her hands—her own preoccupations, what she already knows about the person she's working on, even her assumptions about how the muscles should feel. True, her knowledge of body structure as well as previous experience working on the person help frame this experience, but what ultimately allows the healing moment is the intuitive insight her fingers provide.

Once we have received the whole of the experience, as Langer describes "in embryo," we *search for—or it just comes to us—an image which expresses this wholeness*. My masseuse friend, for instance, described a releasing clump of tension as "a yawn." Because the intuitive moment is so fleeting and ineffable, any desire to reflect upon it or to communicate it compels some kind of symbolic expression. This image or symbol is not like a sign, fixed in meaning. It is mysterious, irreducible to any one interpretation, multi-leveled, flexible.

A recognition of the coherence of these two stages, realization and expression, can be found in the African language Mande-kan which uses the same word, *woron* for "getting to the kernel" and for proficiency in the arts. The achievement of both requires:

> stripping away the superficial covering by discovering its inner and true nature, as in the poetic concept of yere-wolo (giving birth to yourself), in which a person finds his or her... true essence (Thompson, 196).

Although a realization of wholeness does not in itself require symbolic expression, finding that image or symbol can deepen the insight:

> Symbols by their nature can resolve paradoxes and create order from disorder... They provide in flashes of insight knowledge which joins dispersed, disparate fragments in a unitary vision. Thus, symbols, in their function change [us] (Samuels, 82).

Expressing this wholeness through a symbol may in itself be sufficient, or it may lead to a further stage, telling the story which follows from it or playing the music which flows out of it. This process can happen naturally in dreams.

Such a story need not be the traditional heroic story of a person gaining control over nature, context, or matrix. Imagine the seed dropping into the earth: its growth from bud to blossom makes a narration; its unfolding is a potential story. This can be an exciting story in itself if you actually become the seed and contemplate survival and growth issues: Will I germinate? Uh oh, I'm breaking open. What's this sprouting out of me? Why am I splitting apart? I've changed form. Am I still me? Will the frost nip me in the bud? Will bugs chew on me? Will animals tromp on me? Do the gardeners consider me a weed? Will someone pick me?

At any stage of this intuitive process, but particularly as the symbol is dynamically expressed through story, another aspect of the intuitive process becomes possible: transformation. If a symbol is vital, it will be dynamic, not the stable unity represented by a mandala, but the changing unity of a kaleidoscope. This innovation within continuity offers many opportunities, sometimes on several levels, for transformation.

With this transformation can come healing. To see things whole offers a possibility of making things whole again. A kaleidoscope makes whole patterns out of fragments of glass. A quilt creates unity from cast off remnants.

At each stage of this intuitive process we can realize a wholeness, and healing can take place. One person might realize a synthesis of parts that had seemed incompatible. Out of a fuller vision, another person might shed aspects that are too constricting. Still others might integrate elements that are repressed, unconscious or psychic: the left side (left behind, sinister, shadow), the back side, other side, underside, inside and flip sides of life.

The next—I hesitate to say last with this nonlinear process—stage of this process is expansion. There are two ways intuition allows for expansion. One occurs when the symbol itself, along with its story, expands and deepens in meaning. It becomes, in Jungian terms, even more numinous and dynamic. Its full meaning may take years to reveal itself. Out of such symbols, myths are born.

While this storytelling phase might seem quite natural to psychologists or creative artists, it also has relevance for scientists. As feminist anthropologists and biologists have discovered, it is not enough just to observe the behaviors of other people, other realities. We must also be willing to listen to their autobiographies, their stories. Narrative, then, is a kind of process analysis turned inside out.

In "Science and the Unconscious" Marie-Louise von Franz claims:

> most of the basic concepts of physics (such as space, time, matter, energy, continuum or field, particle, etc.) were originally intuitive, semi-mythological, archetypal ideas of the old Greek philosophers (Jung, *M&HS*, 380).

Whether or not one agrees with her, there is no denying that many creative scientists originally conceived of their hypotheses in intuitive flashes. While the scientific method then measures, objectifies, tests and documents such hypotheses, with not much room for intuition, it's clear that very little if any new ground would be broken by scientific method without those flashes.

As feminist critiques of science have shown us about the gendering of such "objective" realities as hormones and bacteria, even the most microscopic dimensions are not only being described in discursive language but also, perhaps unconsciously, being described in intuitive language. Studies like Emily Martin's of the hidden metaphors in medical discourse show how important it is that we bring our own intuitive imagery to the study of our bodies and of our environment.

The second way intuition allows our symbols to expand occurs when we tell our story in the context of other stories so that it extends to a wider meaning and application without generalization, categorization or uniformity. Those of us in the women's movement who participated in consciousness-raising groups know how expansive and transformative such "speaking the plural" can be. As William James describes, such experiences put us in touch with:

> the fact that the conscious person is continuous with a wider self through which saving experiences come (131).

Although he was speaking more of spirit than community, I think it can be argued that the same spirit moves through this experience of the "We of Me."

If telling your story is like dropping a pebble in a pond and watching its effects spread out in ever widening circles, imagine what it would be like if a group of people stood around the edges of a pond and simultaneously dropped pebbles. Each one's widening circles would intersect, without disruption, the circles of the others until eventually they would all form one large, encompassing circle—for a moment. This large circle is similar in transformative power to the great sound of the universe, *OM*, when it is chanted by a group of people. Or we can picture how in Indian art, flower forms unfold and multiply until one huge mandala is formed which maintains the uniqueness and beauty of each separate blossom within the whole.

Within this expanded whole, we see larger patterns, connections, continua which we could not see from the boundaries of our own personal experience. Our horizons have expanded, but we do not lose touch with our own unique, individual experience.

Nor is the multiplicity of many experiences erased by the expansion. This is neither the oneness of abstract generalization nor the unitary vision of mysticism.

A wonderful example of intuitive process and language can be found in the "speaking with names" of the Western Apache. One of the practitioners of this art, Lola Machuse, describes a particular conversation in which she and others were offering comfort and guidance to a distressed friend without judgment or embarrassment:

> We gave [her] pictures to work on in her mind. We didn't speak too much to her. We didn't hold her down. That way she could travel in her mind. She could add on to them [i.e. the pictures] easily (Greenbie, 139).

The pictures they gave to their sad friend were through placenames. These invited the woman to journey imaginatively to places which had been named by the ancestors so she could stand where they did and know what happened there, hearing their voices telling those stories.

> She could reknow the wisdom of our ancestors. We call it speaking with names. Placenames are all we need for that... That woman was too sad... So we tried to make her feel better.

The conversation, as recorded by Barrie Greenbie, consisted, in fact, almost entirely of placenames:

> It happened at line of white rocks extends upwards and out.... It happened at whiteness spreads out descending to water.... It happened at trail extends across a long red ridge with alder trees.

The intuitive connection between the external observation of the landscape and the internal experience of the speakers evoked a tribal story which provided pictures for the listener's own imagination to work with. She could then travel in her mind to her own intuitive realizations. The result in this case was healing for the listener. The stories evoked by the descriptions not only offered her optional scripts, they connected her with a larger context. She was sustained by both the wisdom of the ancestors and the interpretations offered by the supportive community around her. As Greenbie comments:

> Landscapes are available in symbolic terms...and so, chiefly through the manifold agencies of speech, they can be "de-

tached" from their fixed spatial moorings and transformed into instruments of thought (142).

Here there is no division between the subjective and the objective:

Every occasion of "speaking" provides tangible evidence of "thinking," and thinking, which Apaches describe as an intermittent and variably intense activity, occurs in the form of "pictures" that persons "see" in their minds (152).

And here there is no division between the act of imagination and the act of healing:

Western Apache people report that sometimes they do feel better [afterward]. Having pictured distant places and dwelled on distant events, their worries become less plaguing and acute (161).

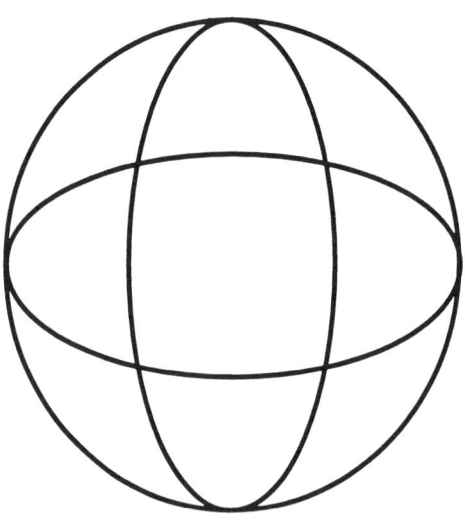

In mainstream American culture people are so used to dualistic thinking that it is hard not to see objective and subjective knowing as opposites. But in the intuitive moment, these two points must interact. Picture a round picture frame. Imagine that it frames, photographically, an objective whole: a portrait, a landscape, a still life. Then picture a hoop of the same size circling it vertically at a right angle. This represents the subjective connection between the viewer and the viewed, the knower and the known. To complete this globe, imagine a third hoop circling both of these in a horizontal direction. This represents the communal dimension, what happens to an intuitive insight when it is shared, as with the Apache "speaking with names." When these dimensions are brought together they form a globe which describes the wholeness of the intuitive process.

In stretching out this intuitive process for the purpose of analysis, I have, perhaps, lost the sense of paradox and simultaneity which is at the heart of intuition. So let me pause now to emphasize how with intuition the mind is both rooted in the specific and capable of remarkable expansion.

This paradoxical quality of intuition is described beautifully by the image from Mahayana Buddhism of the universe as a vast net of jewels, "wherein the reflection from one jewel is contained in all jewels, and the reflections of all are contained in each" (Wilbur, 40).

EXERCISE:
Story Telling, Intuitive Style

To give a fuller understanding of an intuitive process, I offer this exercise:

It is important to keep in mind that there is no right or wrong way to do this. Even though you will be asked to color and to write, no special skill is required. No one will be judging the results. Allow for playfulness, maybe even a surprise or two. Follow your own line of development. If some suggestion from the general framework doesn't fit where your imagination is taking you, just disregard the suggestion—without wasting energy fighting it—and follow your own imagination. Be assured, the results of this process are private; sharing will be optional and under your control.

Think of an issue, problem, conflict, situation, vision into which you would like to gain more insight. It need not be profound—it can be as mundane as the failing clutch in your car—as long as you are willing to follow it to its fullest symbolic or emotional blossoming. One caution though: try not, at this point, to choose someone else's problem, issue or conflict. Make sure it's truly your own. If necessary, reframe it so you are at the center: not "How can I get Johnny to stop drinking?" but "Why do I end up taking care of people like Johnny?"

Now enter into, or drop into this situation. How does it feel? Allow for a full play of emotion, if that is what emerges. Or for a full range of sensations, if those are the primary feelings.

Next, look around. What do you see?

What have you dropped into? Here I will suggest possible images, but of course feel free to find one which is most appropriate for your particular situation. Is it a seed? a tree? a shell? a rock? a cave? a nest?

a house? a scene? a musical? a board game? a playing field? a war zone? a nutshell? or something else?

Now circle around so you can see all sides of it. What do you see? You might want to consider the north (winter), east (spring), south (summer) and west (fall) sides of it, as well as top and bottom.

Is it part of a larger whole? How much of that larger whole can you see?

Now return your awareness to the center of it, where you are, and allow the strongest, most intense, most insistent feeling to emerge (whatever it may be, no censorship necessary).

Feel this feeling, listen to it, give it voice (privately in your head if you are with others, aloud if you are alone and find that helpful). After you have listened to this feeling for awhile, try to record its voice directly, in its own words (or if it doesn't use words, whatever sounds it makes). Don't hesitate to exaggerate. Record this in writing or on a tape.

Now listen for the slightest, tiniest or quietest feeling you can distinguish and find an image to describe its voice: the wind, a plant, a bug, an animal, a kind of instrument or machine, whatever image comes to mind and seems fitting.

Draw a picture of this image, using colors. What is key here is shape and color, not the accuracy of your drawing. Stick figures are fine. A childlike playfulness is useful.

You now have two characters: one powerful enough to have a voice and one distinctive enough to evoke an image. Imagine each as full persons. You may, if you wish, just animate or personify the image (a talking Subaru, for instance), or you can imagine a (Subaru type) personality. What do they look like (tone of voice, gestures, clothing)? What are their personality traits? What are their strengths and weaknesses? What are their names? You can expand these images either through drawings or through written notes.

Imagine a brief interaction between them: who makes the first move, their gestures and body language, actual dialogue.

Now, please, look through a book illustrating mythical characters (you may use illustrations from fairy tales, the Bible, mythologies) or a deck of Tarot cards. Now choose one illustration or card. This can represent another character or a particular situation or scene in this drama—an ally, a guide, an opponent, an obstacle, a magical setting. If this is another character, feel free to give her or him a new name (not just the label on the card). You need not incorporate everything on the card into your story; choose any elements which seem meaningful or relevant.

Now while you play some music, preferably instrumental (words tend to distract from or dictate the process), to help guide or inspire you, please imagine a story which involves these two or three characters and/or scene. (If the music interferes with your process, trust silence instead.)

Your story doesn't have to be coherent at this point.

Instead of forcing a plot or controlling the narrative, just allow options to play through your consciousness: scenes, dialogue, new developments, new characters. Let it depart from the original context as much as it wants to. That particular situation you will have to return to. The story, however, can take you beyond that situation to new horizons, possibly new options.

I suggest that you play the music for ten to fifteen minutes after taking a few deep breaths, relaxing, closing your eyes and allowing a safe receptivity.

Now please summarize your story in writing (or a series of drawings) using whatever dialogue, characterization or description seems called for.

This story can involve mostly action or mostly interaction between the characters. If you get stuck, draw at random another card from the tarot deck or an image from another source and see if you can integrate that new element into the story. Allow for some surprises.

The form of this story need not be formal or high falutin'; it can be a children's story, a folk tale, a segment of a soap opera, a mystery, a TV sit-com, a sci-fi movie script, a comic strip, whatever kind of narrative fits and feels comfortable.

If you are in a group, you might want to take time now to share stories—or whatever part of the process you might like to comment on or get feedback about. On your own or with others, discuss your story in light of the original situation or issue which prompted it. Do they shed light on each other?

If you give it space and some attention, this story can expand in meaning for you. It may surface in your dreams. It may transform itself.

CHAPTER TWO

What is Intuition?

To these elementary laws there leads no logical path, but only intuition, supported by being sympathetically in touch with experience. (Einstein)

A Sufi Tale

ONCE UPON a time a very pious dervish (a dervish in the Sufi tradition is a religious, sometimes holy person) was walking along a river bank, concentrating on how he could become even more pious, when he overheard someone chanting the dervish call.

"Oh dear," he said to himself, "what a waste. That person is mispronouncing the syllables. Instead of intoning 'Ah Ha,' he is saying 'U Ah Ha.'"

Realizing he had a duty, as a more advanced student, to correct this unfortunate person, who perhaps because of living out in the country had no opportunity for the proper guidance, he rented a boat and rowed to the island in midstream where the sound seemed to come from.

There in a crude hut he found a person dressed as a dervish chanting the phrase "U Ah Ha."

"My dear friend," said the first dervish, "I must tell you since there is merit in giving as well as receiving advice—that you are mispronouncing the chant. This is how you say it: 'Ah Ha.'"

"Thank you," said the other dervish humbly.

Full of satisfaction at having done a good deed, the first dervish rowed back toward shore, reflecting on the wisdom that whoever repeated the sacred formula correctly could walk upon the water. He'd never heard of anyone actually doing this, but he had a secret desire to achieve it himself.

At first he heard nothing from the hut, but he was sure his lesson had been well taken. Then he heard a faltering U Ah Ha as the second dervish made the same old mistake, giving the first dervish occasion to reflect upon the backwardness of humanity and its persistence in error.

Then suddenly he saw a strange sight. From the island the other dervish was coming toward him, walking on the surface of the water. Amazed, he stopped rowing.

She walked up to him and said, "Friend, I'm sorry to bother you, but I have come out to ask again the correct pronunciation. I'm having trouble remembering it." Adapted from Idries Shaw (*Tales of the Dervishes*, 63).

Although this Sufi tale can be applied to many situations, I want to apply it here to intuition, that magical ability we all have, that "lost" power we use frequently but don't value because we're intimidated by the supposedly more correct, more rational analysis, linear logic or instrumental thinking.

Intuition, *realization of wholeness(es) which is simultaneously internal and external*, is, as Ursula LeGuin describes it in *The Left Hand of Darkness*: "the power of seeing (if only for a flash) everything at once: seeing whole" (204).

This is not just a sense perception, not even a "sixth sense" which synthesizes other senses. It is an insight which connects both internal and external ways of knowing. Its grasp of meaningful wholeness depends on this fundamental union of subject and object, if only for a moment.

When others use the words *intuit* or *intuition*, they may mean psychic perception, subjective knowing, the unconscious, instinct, mysticism, the right-side of the brain, imagination, active imagination or a sensitivity to possibilities. Although my use of the term shares characteristics with each of these, it is not the same as any of them. I explain some of these distinctions in the last chapter of this book.

One of the most pervasive misconceptions about intuition is that because it moves from "Aha" to the process of figuring out steps 1, 2, 3 of how it reached the insight, then it is irrational. This, despite the fact that most accounts of discoveries by geniuses from composers (Mozart) to scientists (Einstein) describe a crucial moment in their process, illumination, as occurring before rather than after they understood how they arrived there.

The official rational process in the general understanding of scientific method and sound reasoning is to proceed 1, 2, 3, "Aha." Then we have the security of knowing why we know something. Whenever people know something but don't know why they know it, they tend to say they intuited it. But on second thought we understand that much of our knowledge springs from sources we cannot analyze in terms of cause and effect: instinct, sensation, some emotions, psychic awareness, spiritual experience. But not all of this knowing is intuitive. Not all of this knowledge gives us a realization of wholeness.

Intuition arrives at its realization of wholeness from a different route from either abstract generalization or scientific measurement. While the event of intuition necessarily occurs during both philosophical and scientific inquiry, intuitive method is quite distinct from either discourse in that it is narrative, experiential and symbolic.

The way in which the Australian Aboriginal people map their world by way of songlines is intuitive in this way. As such it is profoundly different from either a philosophical reflection on time and distance or a detailed chart of the miles or meters between landmarks. Like the Apache speaking with names, the songlines unite objective knowledge of place and time with the subjective lore of stories and storytellers. The Aborigines sing their way from place to place in a way which locates them historically as well as geographically, giving them both identity and continuity.

One reason we assume intuition is irrational is that we cannot describe it very well in discursive language, the syntax of what we consider rational. Although we can talk about it, as I am trying to do here, that does not make it happen, nor does it really communicate a specific intuition.

As we have seen, intuition cannot be expressed directly through ordinary speech, linear language. It must be symbolic, which allows for simultaneity. Some languages like Chinese, Hebrew and Nsibidi can express more of this symbolic meaning because the actual letters, tones, or ideographs, like runes, are multi-dimensional or mystical as well as discursive. And even more linear languages like English and Italian in the work of poets can take on wholistic reverberations through images, rhymes, puns, rhythms. Emily Dickenson describes this as telling all the Truth "slant."

A brief description of what I mean by image and by symbol might be helpful here. In many instances I use them interchangeably because I view them as two dimensions of a single reality. Imagery refers on one level to a concrete expression of sense (not just visual) experience. At the same time, it also refers to an object of imagination, tangible experience which can be "imaged" and upon which imagination depends. When an image, by way of intuition, becomes charged, expansive and multi dimensional in meaning, it is symbolic. A symbol, therefore, is a meaningful image, but not one fixed in meaning as a sign must be.

Symbolic time seen in a moment, not sequentially, is what Virginia Woolf means by the "expanded moment," an intuitive experience of time which cannot be measured chronologically. It has been called *kairos*, in contrast to chronos. It is what the Tao refers to when it says:

A tree as big as a person's embrace springs from a tiny sprout;
a journey of a thousand miles starts from where your feet stand (93).

Responsibility to this realization of wholeness is expressed in the Great Law of the Iroquois Confederacy:

In every deliberation we must consider the impact of our decision on the next seven generations (9).

A realization of wholeness involves not just expansion in time, past, present and future, but also an awareness of all directions, all sides, including top and bottom. Some say we humans have round heads to enable us to think roundly, globally, wholly. Unfortunately though, with eyes facing forward, many of us are stuck in tunnel vision.

Intuitive awareness requires a different kind of vision from that provided by ordinary eyesight. The Hindus talk about the third eye; we talk about second sight, a reliance on peripheral vision, "eyes in the backs of our heads."

Hearing might be an even better analogy for intuition than vision. As a sense, hearing is multi-directional, allowing for input from all sides, not just the one we're facing. It can be more fully receptive, not so focused on seeing just one thing at a time. Tuned to both tone of voice and music, it allows for greater harmony of impressions. And, according to Dewey, the ear connects with a larger part of the brain than any other sense organ (238).

But comparisons to sense impressions are only metaphors for what is actually a deeper insight. Intuitive realization occurs not just when the sound is round but when the roundness strikes both ear and mind. Speaking of the way intuitive insight was understood in ancient India, William Mahony describes how certain people had "transformative genius or *dhi*." They were:

> 'wise, intelligent'...[with] 'sacred knowledge' in the sense of 'the ability to see things as they really are.'

Through intuition (*dhiti*) the sages, visionaries and poets could:

> give an image to—that is, to *imagine*—sacred realities that, for less imaginative people, were invisible (Mahony, 71, 72).

New Brain Theory

Without claiming to be any kind of expert on brain research, I'd like to draw a quick parallel between intuition and the most evolved part of the brain, the frontal lobe. This is also called the prefrontal cortex or, by Paul MacLean in his study of the Triune Brain, the Angelic Brain. He claims that this part of the brain evolved to counter the "ruthlessness" and disregard for species preservation of the neocortex, or rational brain.

The neocortex, or rational brain, is characterized in its functioning by reliance on what is often considered objective knowledge. It depends on external cues, neutrality, abstraction, and technical, even clinical, terminology. Its efficiency requires "psychic numbing," which prevents it from being tuned to the needs of others or of the whole species. It favors a binary or dualistic approach, using polarization, plus and minus, pros and cons, and either/ors (Coulter, 202).

The working of the relatively newer part of the brain (frontal lobe, prefrontal cortex, or Angelic Brain) is characterized, according to MacLean, by empathy, altruism, foresight and ability to grasp the prevailing pattern. It is very strongly linked to the limbic system, or emotional channel of the brain—perhaps even bypassing what MacLean calls the rational brain. It gives us an awareness of a "universal connectedness to all life" (213). It doesn't use a sequential or temporal reasoning strategy but a spatial one which allows several pieces of information to be considered at once. It ponders over the whole picture, how each part affects the others. It works with multivariables, probabilities and possibilities (which requires imagination). It contemplates data on a continuum, not a set of discrete, clear-cut units—what I would call waves, rather than just particles.

Ironically, the best examples I have discovered of this more highly evolved thinking are among indigenous peoples like the Australian Aborigines, the Apache, the Hawaiians, the African Mande, peoples whose cultures have been looked down upon by rationalists as primitive. Without romanticizing these cultures, we must be astonished at the extent to which racism and other forms of discrimination have obscured our ability to recognize our fullest human potential.

The difficulty of communicating this understanding may be one reason it is not fully recognized. The frontal lobe has no direct motor connection to speech but conducts "inner speech," a way of storing and integrating complex ideas. It has great facility with non-linguistic codes, patterns (and, no doubt, symbol systems). So to express or to explain an intuitive pattern in discursive language, we then must go through the rational part of the brain, as we must to some extent even when using narrative.

Although this new brain research is still exploratory, I find it tends to confirm more ancient systems like the Chinese or the Hindu for explaining the role of intuition. I will not rely on it, or any other physical evidence, for validation, but I will from time to time evoke it symbolically for the new mythology of the brain it suggests.

One immediate, more contemporary connection I like to make with MacLean's findings is Susanne Langer's distinction between genius and talent:

> Talent is special ability to express what you can conceive, but genius is the power of conception (*FAF*, 408).

Talent, therefore, require some native ability and some privileged training (art schools, special classes) whereas everyone is potentially a genius because almost everyone has a frontal lobe, wherein resides intuition, the power to conceive.

Whether we have the talent to express these conceptions or whether they are locked up in inner speech, we share the potential for wholistic realization.

Ironically, Eurocentric, middle class men have this potential too, even though it probably is not as highly developed in them as it is, say, in indigenous women. The current attraction to certain practices of indigenous cultures, from sweat lodges and drumming circles to shamanic journeys, is a measure of the hunger of people in Eurocentric cultures for intuitive methods. There is much we can learn about intuition from cultures which honor that experience more fully. But if Langer is right, we need not appropriate other people's customs to discover our own forms of genius.

In discussions of the brain, one more realm is associated with intuition: the right side of the brain. Popular belief is that its functioning makes intuition possible. Philip Goldberg's argument, "Right Brain, Wrong Theory" (115), against this assumption that intuition resides in the right hemisphere is so thorough and convincing, I won't reproduce it here. He quotes the director of the laboratory for cognitive psychology at SUNY Purchase, Richard Davidson, who says that calling intuition a right brain function is:

> utterly simplistic and inaccurate, an attempt to find an easy answer to what is in all likelihood a fantastically complicated function (116).

What strikes me, when I deconstruct this concept of the right brain, is the synchronicity between the popularity of the theory of the two hemispheres and the rise of political movements for equality, particularly the civil rights movement and the women's liberation movement. Before these movements the dominant culture was characterized by a hierarchy of rational (verbalizing and categorizing) above irrational (emotions, patterns, and images), with the latter, the bottom side, projected onto the underclasses of women and people of color. After those movements we developed a separate but equal theory, with right side and left side both parts of a single brain. Metaphorically our brains corresponded to our raised consciousness.

We tended to ignore the disquieting, because non-validating, research which suggested that males might be more tuned to spatial patterns, right brained, and females more verbal, left brained. Suddenly what had been left behind, devalued, maybe even sinister, was turned around, was right. Many progressive people, myself included, even leftists, wanted then to be considered or to become right-brained. The underdog had become our left-hand woman.

So now, even though the actual research is much more cautious and contradictory, I am left with this new blueprint of the brain. In my personal cosmology what I imagine is a split landscape: on the left hand, right side, a stream of consciousness flowing with images, feelings, patterns; on the right hand, left side, a computer center, capable of measuring, categorizing and naming virtually everything flowing in that stream (if it would just stand still long enough to be labeled).

But in neither realm do I find what I define as intuition, the capacity to fish something out of that stream that will symbolically express and transform experience; the ability to pull pieces out of those cubbyholes and put them together into a meaningful whole. Intuition must draw on both these areas of the human mind for its realization of the whole.

I am reminded here of a film about an anthropologist recording a native culture in South America. Intent on measuring every phenomenon, literally, he tromps around with a tool box full of measuring devices. To help him hold the tape measure as he documents the dimensions of the fields, the spaces between rows, he enlists the assistance of the kind, curious men in the village. While the men are pleased to be playing this game with him, the women are furious that their co-workers are thus lured from the work of helping in the fields. In one amusing intuitive moment, the camera captures a scene of the anthropologist lost in the act of writing down meters, oblivious to the conflict in the background—the women shouting at the men to get to work while the men tease back that they're too busy helping the foreigner.

On the one side is the business of measuring; on the other side is the emotional exchange. And seeing both of them together, within the larger context of green mountains and an indifferent sky, is the intuitive creativity of the film maker.

Models of Cognitive Development

Another construct within which intuition has been examined is the model of cognitive (and moral) development. Various models have been designed by such theorists as Piaget, Kohlberg, Perry and Belenky, Clinchy, Goldberger and Tarule. These models assess and describe steps or stages of development arranged like an ascending stairway. Intuitively I am wary of such linear, hierarchical models and fault them for often ignoring a class bias, even those trying to correct the gender bias. Nonetheless, I realize they have yielded valuable insights into issues of growth and change and have stimulated important discussions for education and therapy.

In the model presented by *Women's Ways of Knowing*, the one most compatible with a feminist perspective, intuition is presented, respectfully, as part of stage three thinking: subjective knowledge, a perspective from which truth and knowledge are conceived of as personal, private, and subjectively known or intuited (15).

This rescues women's thinking from previous devaluation, but it still leaves intuition in a dubious position, despite the disclaimers:

> It is generally assumed that intuitive knowledge is more primitive, therefore less valuable, than so-called objective modes of knowing (6).

Intuition, as I define it, is actually closer to what *Women's Ways of Knowing* describes as "higher" forms of cognition: stage four, connected knowing, and stage five, constructed knowledge. The one who empathizes, the one who understands the importance of context and how frames of reference are constructed, the passionate knower are more than likely also intuitive.

But the intuitive process is not as stage specific or as hierarchic as this model suggests. It often arrives at an insight by going backward, downward, not up, by way of the subjective, the personal, the mysterious; or outward, by way of the communal, the world of nature, the cosmos. While the authors acknowledge the role of empathy in this process, they are constricted within a construct adapted from a rational, linear model. This framework prevents them from exploring in depth how women and other persons cut off from the "higher" levels of privileged thought can arrive, through experiences of loss, vulnerability, dependence, humility and powerlessness, at deeper and more expansive insights than those who are cushioned from such experiences. The symbolic language of the current women's movement is full of descent images, of stories about going down into self, into other worlds.

One clue to how some people can arrive at more "evolved" ways of thinking while going down the stairs or behind the staircase instead of up the pyramid is the intuitive process. Intuition does not require either loss of self or loss of control, and in fact depends upon a fluid core of identity. Nonetheless, an openness to intuitive insight does involve a loosening of the grip of individual ego. Expansion beyond ego may not be considered a stage of cognitive development, but it may, as various spiritual disciplines suggest, be a necessary condition for fuller growth. Intuition is a cognitive process, but not one which can be separated from other growth processes.

An Experience of Intuition

Before writing any further about intuition, I invite you to experience it. Whether or not you believe you are intuitive, you will discover, I hope, that this experience is more a reminder than a revelation. On some level you probably already know what intuition is. All you need do now to make that discovery is relax, close your eyes (after you finish reading this part) and allow something to happen rather than will it to happen. As you close your eyes, try focusing inward, keeping in mind the blind prophet who sees all or the wise sybil in the darkness of her underground cavern.

First bring your awareness to your left foot. Feel how it feels: pressure, tension, temperature and so on. Then follow this awareness up into the rest of your body until you have scanned all parts of your physical self.

Next bring your focus back to your left foot and start erasing that foot, again following that process to erase your whole body. You can imagine holding an actual eraser, blackboard, pencil or art eraser, or you can imagine using a magic wand. If any parts of your body resist erasure, just note which ones and move on to the rest of your body.

Once you have erased your physical self, pause for a moment to feel what is left, what consciousness, what energy. Even without the boundaries of your physical self, you still exist.

Now imagine that consciousness, that energy taking another form. This can be any form, a bird, a cat, a rock, a tree, a cloud, a galaxy. Allow images to shift through your head until you find one that fits who you are and how you feel right now.

After you have found and experienced this new form, return your consciousness to your bodily form and describe briefly how you experienced this exercise. What parts of your body resisted erasure? These parts need, perhaps, some special attention to ease their tension, or they may be parts with which you are most identified. How did it feel to be without physical form? What new form or forms did your energy choose to take?

If there are more than one of you, you may want to share your experience with the others.

Now what is intuitive about the experience you had once you erased your body?

1. First, it allowed a connection to occur between your experience of self and your perception of something outside yourself, in this case a perception remembered or imagined. That connection may

have allowed a realization to occur which illuminated both the subjective and the objective dimensions of your insight. In other words, what you discovered about yourself as a heron or a tornado told you something about how you are feeling, maybe even who you are, at the same time as it gave you a deeper experience of what it might be like to wade and fish or to whirl and roar.

2. Second, this experience relied on an image, the form your energy took in your imagination. This metaphor allowed an expansion of meaning beyond your own self-definition, in this instance the boundary of your physical self. Because it is not just an analogy, which is the symbolic at the service of the discursive, this image provided an illumination which shone both ways, inward and outward, simultaneously. More reciprocal, more like friendship than service.

3. Third, it had a spontaneous quality: a flash, a leap, playfulness, some surprise. Yet it was actually prepared for by relaxation, in this case a meditation on the body. This meditation not only provided the optimum condition for intuition but also allowed for a certain distraction, a lack of focus which intuition (in contrast to discursive reasoning) thrives upon.

4. Fourth, the intuitive experience, if one occurred, was accompanied by a certainty. Once you get an image that works, you know you've got it (which is not to say that everyone will get one that works, at least not right away). This confidence makes it possible to know something without knowing why you know it. You know because you have actually realized it. The image works because it is infused with your own energy, shaped by your spirit, tuned to how you are actually feeling.

And it works well if it is also infused with the energy and dynamism of an authentic external reality, with its own individual and unique characteristics. It works best if it is not a sentimental or stereotypic image but a fully observed or deeply imagined reality.

5. Fifth, it had the quality of synthesis, a both/and experience. You were still yourself, and yet you could also become the bird or the cloud. This synthesis can be followed by analysis, linear thinking and exploration of meaning without destroying the original identification. Intuition tends to see connections rather than make distinctions. Instead of explaining why humans can't fly, intuition imagines how we can, and do, fly.

Descriptions of the Experience of Intuition

[Intuition] is marked by a sense of knowing or understanding patterns and relationships and order where none appeared to exist before (Frances Vaughn, *Awakening Intuition*, 92).

He remembered, not...a logical succession of things, but everything, the whole thing, perfect, complete, in all its dimensions as it were and instantaneously... He no longer needed to reason about it, or even to think about it. He knew it (Dorothy Sayers, *Whose Body?*, 127).

"Creative" conceptions in philosophy and science come only to persons who are relaxed to the point of reverie. Images and ideas come to us not by set purpose but in flashes, and flashes are intense and illuminating: they set us on fire, only when we are free from special preoccupations (John Dewey, *Art as Experience*, 275).

The process of conception...takes place entirely within the composer's mind and issues in a more or less sudden recognition of the total form to be achieved...the total Gestalt [whole world] presents itself.... Once the essential...form is found, the [whole] piece exists in embryo (Susanne Langer, *Feeling and Form*, 121).

We become intuitively receptive to the essence of a symbolic image by holding it steadily in our mind.... Such contemplation... may lead to an identification...[which] enables us to understand symbols from within, and intuition is...the understanding from within of the formless reality which the symbol represents (Piero Ferrucci, *What We May Be*, 119).

[Einstein] was led to relativity by imaging the visual experience of a traveler on a beam of light (Evelyn Fox Keller, *A Feeling for the Organism*, 151).

An experience is a whole and carries with it its own individualizing quality and self-sufficiency (Dewey, 35).

To draw a circle I use my body as a compass. It's off scale. It's like clothing. It fits my body. The gesture and the image are one. The scale is the size of my gesture, human scale, based on my size (Pat Spears, artist, transcribed from a radio interview, WJHU, Baltimore).

Philosophies marked by bias in favor of universal natures and characters have always regarded only the eternal and unchanging as truly real (Dewey, 288).

While the mind grasps knowledge in a mediated way (through words, concepts, mental models, memories, and so on) and analytically, intuition seizes truth in a more immediate and global manner. For this to happen, the mind must become at least temporarily silent (Ferrucci, 120).

"When we are attempting to describe a single psychic event, we can do no more than present an honest picture of it from as many angles as possible" (Marie-Louise Von Franz, *Man and His Symbols*, 167).

We want our mystery to be multi layered, not only horizontally explored but vertically, and not only vertically but wholly. We extend; we climb up and down; we wander around large fields; and then we reflect, we seek a reflective, intensive comprehension (Elizabeth Minnich, "Translation: The Eternal Mystery of Change," 3).

As the intuition is activated, the mind gradually is transformed, becoming less an organ of understanding, a function now assumed by the intuition, and more an instrument for verifying, interpreting, formulating, organizing, and communicating knowledge (Ferrucci, 120).

I wasn't outside, I was down there. I was part of the system... I even was able to see the internal parts of the chromosomes.... It surprised me because I actually felt as if I were right down there and these were my friends (Barbara McClintock, in Keller, 117).

Indeed I and Thou are so fluid within this field of participation mystique that there is often no clear sense of objectivity and differences between the psychic boundaries of two persons. The border is not a fixed barrier demarcating a clear sense of individual identity in opposition to the other... Rather the border is permeable, easily penetrated by empathetic sensing of the other (Sylvia Perera, *Descent to the Goddess*,72).

Dreams are metaphors of life situations and as such you can consider them stories you are telling yourself (Vaughn, 124).

The movement is that of an expanding flower or insect... Proust does not get forward, we complain. Why should he? Is there no other line of development in the universe? (Quentin Bell, in Langer, 300).

A peculiar effect of intuition, which accounts for its synthetic character, is that it has spontaneous ramification in several dimensions of an individual's life. A single intuition may often throw light on previously unrelated issues, showing the existence of the same pattern in all of them (Ferrucci, 245).

The further you go in working with intuition, the more its wisdom will be evident in a balance and synthesis of opposites, in the harmonizing of inner and outer experience (Vaughn, 184).

[Symbols] point to [our] need for liberation from any state of being that is too immature, too fixed or final. They concern [our] release from, or transcendence of, any confining pattern of existence as...[we] move toward...a more mature stage (Henderson, *Man and His Symbols*, 146).

You begin to took at it as a whole... It isn't just a stage of this or that. It's what goes on in the whole cycle. So you get a feeling of the whole situation of which this is [only] a component part (McClintock in Keller, 67).

A human...is a part of the whole... He experiences himself, his thoughts and feelings as something separated..., a kind of optical delusion of his consciousness... Our task must be to free ourselves from this prison by widening our circle of compassion to embrace all living creatures and the whole of nature (Albert Einstein, *Out of My Later Years*, 153).

For [McClintock] the smallest details provided the keys to the larger whole. It was her conviction that the closer her focus, the greater her attention to individual detail, the unique characteristics..., the more she could learn about the general principles by which the...plant as a whole was organized (Keller, 101).

The work of art operates to deepen and to raise to great clarity that sense of an enveloping undefined whole that accompanies every normal experience. The whole is then felt as an expansion of ourselves (Dewey, 195).

Your poetry arises by itself when you and the object have become one, when you have plunged deep enough into the object to see something like a hidden light glimmering there (Basho, in Mitchell, 155).

This is a Blossom of the Brain—
A small—italic Seed
Lodged by Design or Happening
The Spirit fructified
(Emily Dickenson, 945).

Part Two
THE PROCESS IN DEPTH

INTUITIVE EXPERIENCE

Introduction

INTUITION IS profoundly experiential. It is, first of all, rooted in personal experience. That grounding is one of the poles which charge it. And, secondly, intuition is itself an experience, an event. Whether that event happens in solitude or community, through exploration or imagination, in the midst of our ordinary lives or through extraordinary means, it must be experienced before it can be turned into communication or action.

This section of the book presents the experience of intuition from the perspective of an individual and from the perspective of a group. In "One Woman's Intuition" I reflect upon my own intuitive experiences. In "Intuition Shared" students from the same class reflect upon their intuitive processes.

My intuitions were consciously intuitive only upon reflection and, as a whole, shared only now. The students were discovering more immediately the intuitive nature of their insights. They were also sharing this process with others going through a similar process. My piece shows the facets of an individual experience; their piece shows the interaction of multiple gems of insight.

CHAPTER THREE

One Woman's Intuition

WHEN I was a child looking for "the rest of the deer," I couldn't see part of the deer without seeing the whole. I couldn't imagine a head without a body. And I didn't yet know that cutting a part away from its whole requires killing it.

Would I have been searching for the rest if I hadn't already experienced the whole of it? Was I looking for Bambi? remembering a trip to the zoo? reassembling a stuffed animal? jumping to conclusions from what I'd seen of dogs and horses and cows? Even without these experiences, would I have known there had to be more to the deer than just a head?

I'm grateful for that story, which I don't personally remember, and for my grandfather's and my mother's understanding and retelling it. As a child, despite the terror of being left behind, I frequently wandered off from the rest of the family, itself always moving, scouting out the rest of things. But only occasionally, because of other pressing needs, did anyone stop to ask me what I was looking for, or what I found. And when they did, it was hard to find words to tell.

Many years ago I wrote a children's story about the Hums. They were round and full of music. A tune would reverberate and expand into one big sphere of a Hum. The Hums, alas, were invaded by the Kwarks, scissor-like creatures who cut them all into pieces and stopped the music. I never finished the story because I couldn't figure any way the Hums and Kwarks could coexist. The situation really seemed hopeless since the Kwarks' whole purpose seemed to be cutting Hums in half. Writing this now may be a way of resolving that dilemma.

To help resolve my own dilemma, I would like to tell the rest of my story. I'm hesitant because telling before has made me feel cut off. Some people are envious, some feel sorry for me and many just don't understand. Like others whose stories are unique and different, and most people's are when you really listen, I'm tempted to smooth over the distinctive shape so it will fit into pre-established slots, so it will seem regular, so people will understand. But this betrays what really happened, so I keep silent. And people assume my experience was just like theirs.

Part of my story is that I moved with my family twenty-two times before I was eighteen. We lived in various parts of the United States and in other countries. When I was eight we lived in Greece; when I was sixteen we lived in Italy; I went away to college for two years in Germany and traveled around Europe during school breaks, and after I graduated from college I spent the summer with my family in Taiwan, returning through Japan and Hawaii.

Some people respond to this partial summary with a "Wow." Some think it must have been fabulous, and some realize it must have been hard. I nod my head to both, and that's usually that. When I tell other military "dependents," they shrug, "Oh yeah," and that's that.

After I left home, I continued to move every two years as if orders were still coming down from the higher ups. Finally I realized I didn't have to keep following that pattern, and I stayed in the same city. But I moved from apartment to apartment as a way to make major changes in my life. Finally my back started giving out from lugging boxes in and out, and I stayed in the same apartment for ten years. From this new perspective, which is more secure, more comfortable than moving around but just as scary in its own way, I can, perhaps, interpret my experience growing up so that it's more comprehensible.

Even though I've experienced this current change in my lifestyle, this novelty of continuity, I have chosen an environment somewhat consistent with the diversity with which I grew up: people speaking different languages, wearing different clothes, practicing different customs, believing in different divinities, living in different dwellings, surrounded by different landscapes. My neighbors claim Laotian, Mexican, African and Irish roots.

I was fortunate. My mother was an Aquarian who grew up, like Dorothy, in Kansas longing for adventure. She treasures cultural differences. My father, who served in the American military, was chosen for foreign assignments because he got along well with different kinds of people. Whenever possible they chose to live with people ("on the economy" as they say in the military) rather than apart from them in safer, uniform American compounds. Mom studied the language, the art, the customs, got to know people. Dad worked with various "opposite numbers," enjoyed food exploits (goats' eyes, slug soup).

I could write my story by describing various houses we lived in, the Southwest adobe, the aging Greek stucco, the balconies overlooking Mount Vesuvius and the Bay of Naples, the moat-surrounded fortress on Governor's Island in New York harbor. But that might sound like a travelogue. Wonderful as travelogues are, what I want to explore here are spaces between dwellings, moving through those spaces and connections made inside and outside them.

On a deeper level I could describe the people we got to know. There were the Greek kids we played with, big Yannis, little Yannis; the games they showed us, kicking the can out of the circle; and the farm animals they took care of, the lamb we called Snowball they fattened and, to our distress, ate for Easter, the calf we saw born. Language at that age was not a barrier, though except for my youngest sister we did not know Greek, and they did not know English. We relied at first on a mix of gesture, demonstration and sound. Gradually we developed a common, but limited, language which served us well enough. They didn't know why we were so upset about Snowball; we didn't know why they couldn't afford shoes. But I remember these children better than the American kids we played with when we came back to the States, perhaps because of the differences between us, more likely for the warmth of communicating across those boundaries.

With this experience of diversity, I also searched for some kind of unity. I identified with the Greek olive trees, tough and gnarled in a harsh climate much like the mesquite trees in Arizona. Images of the ocean spoke to images of the desert: vast, empty and sometimes blue.

With other children, making connections was fairly easy. With grown-ups I was more aware of differences: Rosa, the African-American woman in Georgia who took care of me as a baby when my mother was sick with another pregnancy; Charlie, the Mexican-Indian man, who helped my grandfather with the gardening when Pop's arthritis had crippled him, he spoke only Spanish and used to ride us in his wheelbarrow; Minna in Greece who giggled a lot; Sophia who walked with a limp, whose name means wisdom and who spoke many languages; and Guiseppina in Italy whose husband died a year after their marriage; his funeral taught me, an emotional child in a family where there was no room for fear and little time for grief, a lesson about grieving I'll never forget.

What I watched were people's hands. Despite a variety of shades, shapes, textures, nails and paces, their hands provided clues to who they were and how they were feeling. When you're a child, adults' hands are important signposts. As I grew older, I watched people's eyes. What mattered was not how they were framed, shaped or colored, what mattered was the feeling they expressed or didn't express. Often I couldn't understand why they were feeling whatever, but I could recognize it, anger, excitement, fear, mistrust, acceptance, joy.

Once in Greece I wandered off into the fields and came upon an old shepherd tending a sheep who was giving birth. When the lamb finally slid out, we exchanged glances. We obviously weren't feeling the same thing; I was flabbergasted and he certainly was not, but I learned from his gentle eyes that I was safe, like the lamb. Once years later, I was wandering the busy streets of Taipei by myself when I looked into the wrinkled face of a man eating rice with chopsticks. Having struggled with chopsticks since my arrival, I was fascinated with his technique, how he held the bowl close to his mouth and used the chopsticks together like a speedy spoon. Suddenly realizing it was probably rude to stare like that, I glanced at his eyes. The twinkle I discovered there suggested he was just as intrigued and amused by me as I was by him. We smiled at each other.

These connections we made were not based on sameness. They were exchanges of energy rather than instances of one of us conforming to the other. Even though I haven't told anybody about them, I remember them. Why? It seems to me now that the greater the differences between two beings, the more charged the experience when that intuitive spark of recognition flashes between them. The more we seek out mirror images of ourselves, the less likely that we will experience such potent bridging between self and other. When I feel such a connection between myself and a terrified baby raccoon or a prism of dew on a spider web or the sway of a hemlock rooted on rock, I know that spark is genuine. It has leapt across some rather obvious differences. As a result the experience can be more fruitful and more exciting than interacting with another whose identity is familiar and comfortable, dulled by resemblance.

As I made connections like these, I also experienced how people are cut off and set apart from each other. Growing up, I saw extremes of poverty, not just our friends in Greece without shoes, but also orphans in Hong Kong begging, people in shanty towns throughout the south in the days before super highways pushed all that into the background, one-room adobes in the southwest, slums in Italy, lepers without facial features in Taiwan. Often the juxtaposition of classes was visible, mansions ringed by huts, yachts tied up to wharfs crowded with the homeless. Early on I began to wonder why some people had so much and some so little. I still wonder.

Everywhere we went there was always some group of people looking down on some other group of people, often in layers of threes. The Chinese Nationalists in Taiwan looked down on the Taiwanese, who looked down on the Montagnards, the native people living in the mountains. The Anglos in New Mexico felt superior to the Chicanas, who felt superior to the Indians. Romans lorded it over Neopolitans, who snubbed the *paysani*, country folk. My own roots reflected it: the English persecuted the Irish, who looked down upon the Tinkers. Within my own extended family, there was always someone who was better off than someone else, someone who judged another harshly because of religion, roots or education. This so-called melting pot or American salad still provides ample opportunity for one ingredient to turn up its nose at another.

And, of course, in almost every country, the streets, the plazas, the buses, the temples were full of men. Women were glimpsed hanging up laundry in alleys, cooking in restaurant kitchens, in back rooms, behind windows, in churches draped in black. Even though women were usually confined to the private realm, they often were the ones with whom we shared the most intimacy.

Because I was a foreigner, because I was lucky, because I had a sixth sense about danger and because I knew how to make myself invisible, as female myself, I lived a kind of charmed life in my solitary wandering. But even then in some places I had to position myself on buses to ward off the groping hands, pinching fingers. This usually required a repetitive and rapid chopping motion with my hands.

During long hours of travel in cars, trains, buses and ships, gazing out at shifting horizons, I had ample opportunity to ponder the reality of these splits. Despite the variety of cultures, landscapes and elements, the earth seemed to retain a wholeness. But it seemed that what we humans had most in common was how we are divided.

To cover up that divisiveness there were pressures to conform, from the military, from the church, in school and in the family. My mother delights in the fact that none of her four children is like another, except in "stubbornness and a sense of humor." But traveling with us back and forth across the country and twice across the Atlantic demanded a certain degree of uniformity or, as she preferred to call it, "cooperation." Walking my two dogs on leashes so they won't run out into busy streets, I can appreciate the problem of having everyone run off in different directions. But much as it protects us, conformity also serves to remind us of how different we are.

Along with these experiences of multiplicity, I had many-leveled reminders of my own separateness. Within the family, our one constant, although it split apart and reunited when my father went off to or returned from three different wars, I was an odd bird. As a result I felt more at risk of being kicked out of the nest or flying away than the others, though each of the six of us, being unique, could claim our special brand of alienation.

I also did not wholly identify as American. Like Whitman's child who became a part of all he met, I was by osmosis part Indian, part Greek, part African-American, part Italian, part Chicana, part Chinese. I experienced a large dose of anti-Americanism when we lived in other, particularly European, countries. This split was echoed when I became involved in the anti-war movement and witnessed a great deal of anti-military sentiment. In both instances, I felt torn apart by the judgments, able to sympathize with both sides. I am both proud and ashamed of being an American.

A mix was true of religion as well: my mother was Catholic; my father, Protestant, the only Protestant in our nuclear family. Sometimes I attended Catholic schools where I tuned out the fear of Protestants; sometimes I attended public schools, where I tuned out mockery of the parochial.

I know what it's like to be a minority. A privileged minority: one of the few Anglos in a mostly Chicana school run by Anglo nuns, one of the few white teachers in a black university. An ignored or despised minority: the only woman in all-male faculties, a lesbian in a heterosexual world. And one of a kind not discriminated against: the lone goy, the lone Catholic, the lone American, the lone radical, the lone poet.

Not only are my family roots located in different soils and different classes, in my own life I have experienced financial fluctuations, the shame of both relative wealth and relative poverty. In Taiwan my parents had seven servants, most of whom were spies for the Nationalist government, leaving the others, cook, houseboy, laundress, to do the work and keep us prisoners of luxury. For several years I worked at a temporary, part-time position with no benefits, no health insurance and not enough income to pay taxes, dependent for emergencies on the generosity of family and friends. But this was relative poverty. Compared to the lives of at least eighty percent of the world population, I was lucky.

Categories, labels, judgements and hierarchies: all these turn any positive sense of separateness and uniqueness into alienation. Signs on shut doors: "Colored drinking fountain"; "Americans, go home"; "No women allowed"; "Servants' Entrance"; "Private Property"; "Burn, Faggots, Burn." Such signals, of course, prevent us from looking each other in the eyes, much less holding hands.

I grew up in the context of the worst kind of splitting: war. Even though we were spared the graphics of televised war until Vietnam, during World War II and the Korean War we listened to the radio every night, we played war games, we absorbed our mother's anxiety and our father's post traumatic stress. Not only did war split up our family (our father was with us only half of my growing up years), it split people from people, country from country and, to recall the deer image, heads and legs and arms from bodies. During the Vietnam War, our whole family split apart. Two of us "dependents" served in the war (one building roads and bridges, one working for the Red Cross) while two of us were arrested for protesting against the war (one losing her job as a result). In the aftermath we argued and shouted until we could no longer listen or talk to each other, much less share experiences or purge the bitterness.

The first month after I left our home in Italy to go to college in Germany, my consciousness was blasted with the reality of the consequences of anti-Semitism. The school sponsored a trip to Dachau. On the bus there I was still a child, giggling and flirting. On the way back to campus, I was no longer a child. Standing in the shower room gas chamber, I felt as if I had died there. When I returned to the dorm, I painted a picture of the view from that cellar. Outside, beyond the barred windows, was a newly planted tree, a symbol of hope denied to those who'd been trapped in there only a decade earlier.

Given these realizations, it was hard to remember the poor deer had ever been whole.

Since words, labels, categories seemed so destructive, I reached for images to express my experience. When I was thirteen, I wrote a song about tumbleweed which "longs to sink its roots deep in the heart of land." I studied images of the Wandering Jew, vagabonds, gypsies. I read poems about the Mississippi River, a symbol of both change and continuity.

I found only one place where diversity was honored: Grailville, a women's community on a farm in Ohio sustained by radical Catholic laywomen who belonged to an international organization called the

Grail. Although within the Church, they were, in the fifties and sixties, among the vanguard of today's liberation movement. They were ecumenical, incipiently feminist, actively opposed to racial and economic oppression.

At Grailville in 1962, I lived with and became friends with women like Noriko, an artist from Japan; Regina, a social worker from Portugal; Dorothy, a teacher from Dominica in the Carribean; Ceci, a Native American; Jackie, an Italian-American; Anne, an Irish-American. There were others; I'm naming some of my special friends.

In this context I realized what I hadn't allowed as a dream, becoming an odd bird among other odd birds, being special without diminishing anyone else's specialness. It was the only place I have lived where differences in background made mostly positive differences. Differences which involved privilege were not dealt with openly, however, perhaps because that might have been divisive. I can only conjecture how much difference gender would have made, how possible such an experience would have been if men, before the consciousness-raising of the second wave of feminism, had been there. Places where I have heard faint echoes of this kind of sharing have been in the women's movement, the gay liberation movement and at colloquia and seminars of the Union Institute.

This particular experience of wholeness expanded when I was sent as a delegate to an international Grail conference in Europe. There I got to know women from around the world. This was heaven, not because everyone agreed, lord knows, but because all voices could be heard, for that moment at least.

Although the Grail was affirming of differences, with the significant exception of homosexuality, her father the Church was not. Grailville survived on the fringe of Catholicism. Eventually the rigid hierarchies, a limited role for women and my own questioning of much of what I'd been taught to believe drove me across the threshold of the Church into an undefined outside. I've never been able to escape hierarchical structures, from military ranks to academic ratings, but I also haven't chosen to integrate such structures into my belief systems.

My brief involvement with the Grail propelled me into political action. My priority became helping create opportunities for equality. I knew that plurality was impossible without equality, that honoring multiplicity was a limited reality in the context of any hierarchy, particularly one which reinforced racism and sexism.

Thanks to the Grail, I participated in the March on Washington in

D.C., where Martin Luther King gave his "I Have A Dream" speech. My bluest eyes full of tears were almost lost among the sparkling browns. Since then the mobility of my childhood has transformed into movements for equality, civil rights, worker rights, the right to say "no" to war, women's rights, gay rights.

Looking back over the past twenty-five years, I know we have made progress. The ugliest trappings of segregation have been dismantled: no more facilities for "colored" and "white." Women have more choices: we are no longer confined to unpaid or low-paid labor. I hope our overall consciousness about racism and sexism has been altered in ways that can never be reversed. The abuse of women and children is finally at least being discussed. But hierarchal thinking and the inequalities it supports are still intact. The Capitalist Democratic Hierarchy has been remarkably flexible in allowing token people of color, selected women and closeted gays to rise to the top, fostering the illusion that the top is the place to be. I long for the day when we turn the ladder on its side, stop the futile climbing and instead start talking with each other.

Political consciousness, no matter how liberated, still categorizes people as progressive and reactionary, still demands to know which side we are on. At the level of political action, some kind of reckoning, of commitment, is essential. We must put our lives on the line if we expect to enact justice, equality, compassion. But those of us who are activists know only too well how that line can cut both ways. On the level of personal growth and consciousness, this kind of labeling spawns hypocrisy, guilt and alienation.

Beyond the solidarity of those who share the same convictions, such thinking does not make real connections between people any more than the old categories did, does not recognize the complex facets of each person. It does not ease, but often exacerbates the divisions between and within us. Too often it mirrors the splitting it is attempting to heal. How many progressive organizations I've watched splinter apart out of their own internal dissensions and hierarchical judgments.

I myself am created of multiplicities. Labels, even all strung together (woman, white, middle and working class, teacher, poet and artist, INFP/J, Irish, Capricorn sun and Aries moon, American, feminist, country/city person, aging) do not begin to describe who a person is. Categories and the attempts to combine them: gender (androgynous); ethnicity (a mixed breed); class (neither downwardly mobile nor rising with the cost-of-living); and sexual preference (bisexual) do not touch the complexity of one's background and experience. It would take a multidimensional, multilayered and shifting diagram to chart a single personal identity. And any one life is, more or less, just as complex as any other life.

For my first twenty years, I was jerked around by the military-industrial complex; for the next twenty years, I resisted. At the same time, as a teacher, counselor, editor, I was trying to help people find their own voices, tell their own stories rather than let others name their reality for them. My motto was: no abstraction without representation. For the final trimester of my life I would like to explore how intuition can help us make a wholeness out of our stories.

The Hindus envision the universe as a vast net of jewels, each stone giving out its own light while reflecting the light of every jewel around it. Each gem must be able to glow with its own special brilliance before it can radiate to the others. But unless they are all connected, there are no myriad reflections. Each would shine only for itself. These connections don't result from a single spotlight or a single generator. Nor do they measure a scale from brightest to dimmest. They emerge from mutual exchanges of energy, lights between live eyes.

This vision of the universe, and of a truly free society, is intuitive. It rises from a realization of wholeness which is simultaneously inward and outward. Intuition enables us to see and make connections across vast spaces of difference. It enables us to see wholeness without wiping out diversity and without fixing any one moment into universal meaning or eternal truth.

Because intuition requires a different language, the language of symbolism which speaks through the images of art, dreams and nature, it avoids words which label, categorize, divide, grade and rate. It treasures the unique individual shape and identity; it values multiple realities. Neither art nor nature declares one plant a weed and another a source of beauty or nourishment. The dandelion is condemned only by the way we think about it. Intuition would allow each plant some space in its garden.

Rooted in each person's experience, intuition allows the complexity of that individual to find its own imagery and to expand with its own wholeness. It allows us to empathize with the dandelion and in so doing, perhaps, discover its medicinal properties. Because one of the ways intuition expands is through story, it discovers and creates a narrative continuity which allows for transformation that goes deeper than mere change.

As long as there is time and space for each person to value her or his own experience, find the images that express that experience and tell the stories that grow out of those images, then each voice can be heard. My story does not cancel out yours, nor yours, mine. Sounded together, they can make their own whole.

CHAPTER FOUR

Intuition Shared

THE FOLLOWING comments were culled from the journals of students in one women's studies class on intuition. The course itself will be described in Chapter Seven. This collage of quotes is offered as an example of the sharing of intuitive process and of the insights sparked by that process. Each quote is from a different person. Much as I would like to give credit for these reflections, I have left names out to protect the confidentiality of the class.

Week One:

Some of my fears: I don't want to be part of a group of women who find it necessary to generalize about men and put them down. I find this just as offensive as doing the same to women. I am afraid of things that I don't believe in as a Christian, for example, tarot cards and astrology charts. I like being part of a group of women. I like to hear discussions that go below the surface of a person. I enjoy sharing my thoughts also. I really got into this exercise. I was floating above myself... I then became a bird. I often feel what it must be like to fly.

An image of intuition to me is centering into the core of one's self, one's emotional warehouse, and then letting thought occur. This thought can come in the form of a word, but more likely as a picture, an abstract form that develops into something more recognizable, color, or maybe just an image of an emotion. It was really interesting to see the pictures and hear the relationship of expanding flowers to intuition, interesting because as a child I loved to draw flowers and I always drew them like an expanding flower. Often I would make one that filled a whole page and then spend hours coloring it in. Perhaps

I had been intuitive as a child but was taught to monitor it as I got older.

I spent the majority of my life trying to be everything to everyone, my parents, my employers, my children and my husband. Now I feel I must do what makes me happy. This may be selfish, but if I don't care about myself, who will support my interests?

Week Two:

When the exercise in class was given, the problems of the week were weighing heavily on my mind. My drawing reflected my feelings, as did the cards I selected. I chose the card with the mother hugging her child, while the witch-doctor was threatening near by. I also chose the card with the hens in the yard and a wolf approaching. I couldn't believe it when I found those two cards; they said exactly what I was feeling. When we were reflecting while the music was playing, it seemed like everything just kind of boiled over and I started to cry. It felt good to cry and I wish I had been alone so I could have gone on longer.

There were a lot of eggs and I was dancing on them. They did not break. It was perfect. Then one did break when I danced on it. Everyone looked and pointed. I felt ashamed but there was someone in the next scene who encouraged me to continue to dance. And so I did. I danced and danced and danced. I broke more eggs. I looked at the eggs as I broke them. I did not concern myself with the fact that I broke these eggs. I was happy. As I got to the next scene, the eggs showed life. People came from out of the eggs. They joined in the dance. We had fun. The eggs kept forming life. The people from the eggs kept dancing. They danced in their own direction. We danced in our direction. No problems. No worries. We were happy to be dancing. To break the eggs was at first a mistake. But once a mistake is made, good can still come from it. One mistake does not a failure make. I was very content with this vision.

If the seed were a person, she would be a bit insecure, dress conservatively, have a small voice, be a little scared of life. If the tree were a person, she would be strong and firmly planted, outgoing, have a deep, powerful voice, and willing to try anything that life has to offer. She would have many facets to her personality. I just read over my story from class and was amazed at how clear my thinking was about this whole situation. I have been agonizing about the decision. The exercise in class cleared my mind, focused it on my decision and drew my true feelings to the surface. I was meaning to rewrite the story because I felt it was sloppily written and didn't make much sense, but after reading it now, I wouldn't change a thing and it has given me renewed confidence that what I did was the best thing for me.

Week Three:

Women's intuition? Because, while the idea of intuition is valid, it's kind of like God, it can't be scientifically, rationally explained. So a tag must be put on it to prove it invalid. It makes unbelievers, rational, scientific people, often men, nervous. I'm glad intuition belongs to women. I like having it tacked on to my status.

I especially felt moved by the chanting meditation, first, because I am not used to hearing my own voice make such a sustained, musical sound. Lately I've been conscious of the pain, at times, I feel in my throat. It has pained me to hear this false voice which comes from my mouth that I know is not my own. The meditation gave me the refreshing experience of getting close to my own true sound for that moment. Second, I heard so much healing energy in the myriad of tones voiced by my peers and I was powerfully moved.

Wow, I do this all the time. So this is meditation. I use this tool to center into myself, what is important to me at that time and place, bringing my thoughts and feelings out and giving them 'time' so to speak. If that was 10 minutes, it went by very fast. I had an image of me looking upward into a dome lined with all the responsibilities of my life, such as mother, student, worker, daughter, sister. I just floated there until...a powerful feeling emerged that made me flush and brought tears to my eyes. Where oh where is there time for me? Where do I fit in?

The drawings in class scared me at first because I never considered myself an artistic person, but the ideas and colors and designs just came to me and ended up expressing exactly what I wanted them to. I may even begin drawing what I feel at home now that I have confidence about it. The mandala that I drew was symbolic of trying a number of ways and times to get to a goal and finally reaching it.

My dream poem:
At the base of the stairs
A small child pondered.
The black door at the top
Looked dark and ominous.
What lies beyond the door?
Open the door, open the door!

Another dream poem:
Stains on the wall
pink feathery blotches
like cotton candy
deliberately thrown
spite.

Week Four:

When I speak my voice is deep, all my chambers echo, and I sound like many voices when there is really only one. When I pop open my chambers, it is a very satisfying sound to me, but of course once open they can never close again. Although I am very beautiful when I am green and closed, I am much more interesting when I am old and my chambers are empty. Around my many chambers are protective apparatus which make each chamber difficult to investigate. My function is propagation. Once I have served my purpose I become dry and fragile. I can be carried away on the wind or, laying unnoticed underfoot, easily crushed. I finish my life quite differently than when I am young and green. But even in my old age, I am beautiful; and those who seek me out marvel at the perfection of my purpose and form. My seed will propagate the earth and even as I end my days I know the cycle will continue.

In my dream I wanted to go to the lady in the mirror to tell her to come help. At the same time I watched S. roll over. As she rolled, she left her body. She became four people. Each was herself. Each had their own hairstyle. Each wore a different set of clothes. I watched in awe. Then she rolled back into one person.

I like this exercise. I am aware I have options. It is empowering. Looking more closely I realize I am taking action on some of these matters because they are meaningful to me and I am choosing to do so.

I think the object is saying "I've been through a lot in life before I ended up here. I have cuts and holes, but I'm still in one piece. I have rough edges, but my inner seed is smooth and fresh. I am more calm on the inside than I think."

The visualization of time has always fascinated me. I picture time as a spiral, spiraling outwards. To me that explains why life seems to always be in cycles. It is like the earlier cycle affects the outer circle. I also like to think that things like ghosts are images that are able to pass from one circle to another. I like to think that one day people will be able to pass from one circle to another. The past affects the future but the future also affects the past.

The voice is a deep feminine voice. It is full and musical. It tells me about forming for years in secret and then one day being broken apart and her brilliance being allowed to show.

Week Five:

Across from me is a straight back chair. The uptight business lady walks in. I tell her to leave. She has no words of wisdom for me. She takes her chair with her. Then a lady in silk, billowing scarves of red, yellow, blue, green, comes in. I say, 'Will I?' She says 'Yes.' She understands. She leads me out into a jungle with vines and big green leaves and I dance in them. I am safe and I am happy.

As I read what I wrote last Saturday, I am amazed with my imagination. I never thought of myself as a creative person, but I really feel like what I wrote was pretty powerful and to think that the wise woman is in me somewhere and I never knew it. I showed my mom and my sister what I wrote and they were fascinated. I'm fascinated. I can't believe that came out of me. The whole experience just seems to have come from a remote place in myself that I have never discovered. I didn't think about what I was writing. I just retold the story, as it happened, a few minutes later. The words just flowed out, I didn't have to think about what I was writing at all. It took me a while to really understood what I had written—what I meant by what I said. The whole experience has alerted me to a whole other side of myself and a whole new way of thinking about my world. Trivial things mean relatively nothing in the great scheme of things. Getting back to nature, becoming a part of the universe again, seeing what's most important in life, these are the things I should be concentrating on, not pointless worries about things that may never happen. I learned a lot from myself Saturday.

I never realized before what an impact my childhood had on me until I began writing my thoughts and dreams down and doing the exercise in class. A central theme is developing and I guess that answers the question of what I will write my creative piece on.

She is older, grey haired, with a deep voice, strong, yet kind and gentle. I asked her what I should do about N. I think she said to go. When we left the crystal, I saw N. as an angel, whole, well, and flying in the sky, she was happy, with open arms, she embraced me, but she was not human. Then my mind began to wander, back to what I must do to get out there to see her before she dies.

Week Six:

After experiencing the dialogue that our volunteers shared in class on the subject of abortion, I was most impressed. Each woman elaborated on the character she chose to develop. This sharing brought forth deep emotion and greater empathy on the subject of abortion. It was an impressive display of how intuition brought better understanding to the class and to the women themselves as they shared and talked. We all became very involved.

Continuing the exercise I have been working with those awful ugly faces that come unbidden when I close my eyes. As Margaret suggested, I waited them out, asked them what they wanted to eat, then took them out in the sunshine, played with them. I used to be very frightened of them, worried that they were a reflection of anger or evil within my self. I have come to realize they are representations of fear within my self.

I have taken some healing steps for my family since I began this class. I feel so good about this I can hardly express my joy.

The exercises in imagery and myth-writing have brought to the surface some strong feelings I have not dealt with for a long time, and I guess it's time to face them. I have chosen to write a modern myth dealing with my childhood and my anger regarding some things that happened with my mother. Perhaps this will give me some insight into the question of why.

All of a sudden I became her [an average-looking lady who suddenly turns into a terrible raging hag], and hideous wrath was all around me like flashes of lightning, and then I returned to my normal self and I understood that she was anger held internally and not allowed to be expressed.

Week Seven:

It was fascinating, my mind dropped right into my grandmother and the words flew. When I finished and reread what I had done, I was pleasantly surprised. Where had the words and feelings come from? Why was I able to write for a grandmother I only knew after she had arteriosclerosis and some dementia had set in? How did I know my grandmother so well?

Before I went to bed I meditated and requested a dream to guide me through the creative project, and to remember. That night I had a dream that was full of images and emotions. When I awoke I felt the need to draw pictures. No matter what I tried to draw, the pictures felt wrong. I invited an artist friend over and I told her about my dream and the images and emotions I experienced. While I talked she started drawing pictures, some thought-provoking, some original, but not right. My gut told me, go back to my original drawings and just let go and enjoy. Don't judge. After awhile the picture did become more like my dream. The images changed some. The colors transformed. But I feel the end result is true to the dream. The main thing I learned from this project was the value in opening up to expression without judging the process or product or outcome." (After sharing this project with the class, this student told of a incident when she was in grade school: the teacher crumpled up her drawing and threw it in the trash because she hadn't done it "right," according to directions.)

This was the greatest class experience of all. Someone made the comment that it was better than opening Christmas presents. I concur. The creative energy that was present during this class was fantastic. The projects were beautiful. Many seeds of creativity were sown at the beginning of the semester. They became a beautiful harvest for us all during this class.

It was wonderful to see everyone's excitement about their projects. It seems that everyone learned an incredible amount from this. I know I did. I was so worried that I wasn't going to be able to create something imaginative (My sister was always the creative one in our family). But my project practically wrote itself, it came right from my heart.

I was able to put into words some very dear memories. I was able to get feelings out, yet keep the essence by writing poetry. I thoroughly enjoyed the writing. To find creative expression was for me like giving birth to part of me. Quite painless though, and very moving.

I have enjoyed this class very much. The class contained a broad mix of women: young women, about to graduate, on the threshold of life; young mothers who are at a different stage in life; lots, like myself, of middle-aged women, some of whom are as confused as myself. Lastly, there were a few older women, wise and full of experience. What a great combination. I really feel we've learned from each other. I know I have. It has been more like meeting with friends rather than attending a class. I'll miss it.

INTUITIVE LANGUAGE

Introduction

TO EXPLORE how intuitive experience is expressed and communicated through intuitive language, I will share three contexts: the play of children, the literary work of women writers and the learning process of students in a women's studies class. Within each of these contexts specific issues about intuition arise, and certain aspects of intuitive language can be observed in depth.

Whenever we play with children, we realize from their ease with intuitive language how natural intuition really is. The way the girls in the Heart Gang or the boys who are super ninjas drop into their imaginations and act out their fantasies illustrates the intuitive process as well as any more sophisticated example.

Children's ease with intuitive language does not mean, however, that they are more inventive with it or that their usage is less tainted by inherited prejudices and stereotypes than the symbolism available to adults. True, their playfulness may imply a certain freedom to pick up and discard symbols like toys. But many symbols, like many toys, are cultural givens, loaded with the belief systems and values of the society into which each child is born. Few children are able, on their own, to challenge these values. If the intuitive process and its accompanying language were allowed greater validity in the process of development from childhood to adulthood, we could more easily stay connected to more authentic experience, discover the most effective way to express it and actively examine and challenge cultural assumptions which negate it.

The second context, the literary work of women, explores how these writers challenge inherited values by transforming given symbols into intuitive language which expresses more truly their experience and the experience of others like them. In particular, I will examine how Ursula LeGuin, Maxine Hong Kingston and Doris

Lessing revitalize established archetypes: yin/yang and the chakras. These symbols resonate for whole cultures but have become fixed in ways which negate or devalue the experience of many people within those cultural systems, particularly women. By reanimating these symbols, the writers bring them into consciousness through an artistic process which also transforms them.

The third context in which intuitive language is used shows how transformative sharing our intuitions in an interactive way can be. The intuitive process is not really complete until the intuition is communicated, either directly or indirectly. In the women's studies classes, women shared not only the results of their intuitive processes, but also the process itself. By bringing these experiences out of separate closets, sharing images and symbols which had been forgotten, no longer fit or had been soiled by everyday use, these women created for each other a context of exchange which encouraged and stimulated each participant while enriching all. An image discarded by one person would prove engaging for another. An issue shared led to variations on a theme.

In many ways an exchange of intuitive language is like any other genuine communication. But because intuition allows us to delve so deeply into our experience and express it with so much integrity, communication between these women happened on a deeper level than ordinary conversation. It certainly went deeper than the usual discourse between strangers in a regular college classroom. This mutual exchange shows how transformative intuitive language can be when it is freed from the artificial and often elitist confines of the gallery and concert hall.

CHAPTER FIVE

The Heart Gang

> In the growing-up process, narrative is both a powerful cultural tool for reinforcing the status quo and a powerful personal tool for shaping individual identity (Frye, 77).

NOT ONLY do children's stories reveal their socialization process, they show how we use intuition to explore personal identity and change. Because intuition is tolerated in them and because they have not yet learned to devalue it, children seem more naturally at ease with image and story than adults. Much of what I've learned about intuitive language comes from what I remember of my own childhood and what I've observed playing with children. These experiences have made me aware of intuitive process, how important playacting is to intuition and where story telling fits into this process.

   Valentine's Day

   When I ask the girls
   what Valentine's means to them
   Jeannie tells about
   a little heart-shaped cookie
   afraid of being eaten,
   who runs away, falls into a mud
   puddle and gets all soggy.

   And Laura says, as she colors
   hearts for cards, "Kissing—
   eeyu, yucky."

"Why hearts?" I ask.
"What do you know about your heart?"
"It makes too much noise,"
Julia replies. "Especially
when the moon is full
and the werewolf comes out."
Her hand over her heart
goes thump, thump, thump.

Several years ago, Lena, my four year old friend and neighbor, came to visit.* As soon as she entered the front room, she started removing figurines from the shelves and placing them on the rug. From this arrangement, as often happened when she was there with her sister, a drama developed. The main characters this time were the king (a representation of Shakespeare's Falstaff) and the daughter/maid (a little girl with a flute, an established favorite, one with whom the girls immediately identified).

On this occasion the figurines provided the parts. On other occasions, characters were chosen differently: "I'll be the poor little girl." "I'm the princess." "I'm the unicorn." Or when watching TV, announcing: "I'm her." While sometimes there is a rivalry over a favorite part, along with negotiation and usually compromise, maybe even sharing, more often each girl has her own palette of roles to try on, sometimes in costume. But regardless of how it's done, one of the first concerns is who is who: the characters.

When I asked why the daughter was the maid, Lena replied it was because she did a lot of work. I realized later she had, with unconscious insight, collapsed two meanings of "maid" into one. But that wasn't the issue she wanted to deal with. The real issue was that the king was mad at the maid. The reasons were unclear, although one possibility seemed to be the fact that she didn't want to go to bed.

Once the drama was set, I could see how distressed Lena was about the king being angry. She often comes to my house when she is upset. One time she was mad at her mother who wanted her to wear pants to church because it was cold. She wanted to wear a dress.

In order to help Lena get in touch with her feelings, I brought out a box of crayons and asked if she wanted to draw some pictures. She was eager. First, she drew a picture of the king. She then drew a very small daughter. I suggested she draw the daughter as she grew up, in stages. She said okay, but later, and went on to draw a whole sheaf of

*Names have been changed "to protect the innocent."

pages about the situation, finishing with a much larger grown-up, powerful-looking daughter. Then we put the pictures in a folder and stapled them together as a book, which she took home to show her family.

Before we did this, she started writing letters on the pictures, trying for words. Since she didn't write that well yet (at four), I asked if she wanted to tell the story into a tape recorder. Interestingly, when she did, the whole story changed and the king was no longer angry. In fact at the end he and the maid got married and lived happily ever after. For a finale, there was a spiritual vision, with lots of singing and heavenly hullabaloo.

Laura

Finally after listening to the tape, she went to the piano and started singing and playing. The music, though somewhat discordant, was original. It sounded like a very modern musical.

Then she took various hats off the hat rack and acted out various characters. Whatever heaviness was with her when she first entered was gone by the time she left.

What struck me was how easily she used the various media to define and solve the emotional dilemma which troubled her. I was also impressed by how easily she flowed from one mode to another. As I followed her process, I saw a certain method evolve. The figurines helped establish and describe the situation. The coloring helped clarify and move the emotion along. The storytelling helped transform the situation. And the music and acting enabled her to fully express the transformed or released emotion (in this case the love which had been held hostage by anger).

Different children will choose different sequences, depending on their individual inclinations, the problem, the context. What is remarkable about the process is how the playacting, the art, the storytelling and the music combine into one whole event of art and healing.

Another time we practiced intuitive transformation. Lena, her sister Jessie and their friend Jennifer were visiting. This had become such a regular occurrence that they started calling themselves The Heart Gang. (This won the vote over Rainbow Club, The Black Panthers, The Hawks, The Pigs That Eat Candy.) Dropping immediately into playacting, they improvised a drama about a snake chasing them. They were squealing, shivering, crawling under the table, dramatically disappearing.

I wondered if this had anything to do with older brothers who teased and chased them. So I suggested a role reversal. "Be the snake." They looked surprised, frightened, then intrigued. Frozen for a moment, their eyes filled with delight. How to be a snake?

"Draw the snake," I suggested. They did. Colors poured out, shaping themselves into snakes.

"What's happening?" I asked Lena when she was done.

"The snake is flying," she sang out, as she sailed off home, vibrance intact, to show off her picture.

They transformed the situation by identifying with the energy instead of running away. Lena had, furthermore, transformed the snake by adding wings, unknowingly evoking the ancient symbol of the snake/bird goddess.

Although I guided this particular transformation, the process was not new to them. What I learned from the children about intuition is how easily they can drop into an experience through playacting, especially girls. (Boys do it too, but they seem more reluctant to allow grown-ups to witness their pretending.) In some ways coloring is a more focused form of play acting. "Let's pretend" we are whatever we're drawing. Unlike most adults, children can just as easily switch roles as drop into one. Parts they play are parts of a whole they can pretend to be, despite already constricting stereotypes of gender and class. The intuitive pull to become the experience is as natural to them as giggling. Here is where their emotions are easily expressed, here is where they feel the excitement of creativity.

Adults remember the power of this mode when involved in psychodrama or improvisation. Playacting, pretending, allows an integration of feeling and imagination that blasts through carefully constructed adult masks and poses. Drama has an immediacy that narration does not. Each serves an important function within the intuitive process.

When children are young, playacting seems a more natural mode than story telling. Dawn, a child of three, for example, told this story:

Once upon a time a big bear came and then he ate up all my keys and then he just went away. And then a real bear came and then he wanted me to ride on his back and then I did. And then he flied up the air fast. He did that really fast. And so he just came and ate me and all my teeth up. "Hi, Joe, I'm just going to go fishing now." That's the end of my story.

The same child would play act this script for days and days: being scared of the bear, being the bear, riding the bear, flying, being eaten up by the bear. Some other children I know played variations of The Wolf and Santa Claus for at least a month before Christmas. (The game consisted of having someone hide behind a curtain and then emerge, either as the Wolf, which necessitated screaming and running away, or as Santa, which involved the giving of presents.)

What usually matters at this age is depth, variety and fullness of experience, not continuity. Children playing together will create an infinitely flexible story line, which serves as a common ground rather than an established plot, although they also readily play with or borrow from given plots.

For children who have been moved around a lot, however, continuity becomes more critical. One four year old, almost as soon as we got to know each other, told me the story of her birth by drawing a picture of an arc of a plane flying across the world. She was adopted at six months and transferred from a foster home in Korea to her new home in Baltimore. For her the flight was her birth: the passage to her mother.

As children get older, the issue of continuity becomes more crucial and more possible. Stories take on a new importance. First, they are inherited scripts, stories told by grown-ups, records of what went on before they arrived on the scene. But they also help pull together the disparate events and separate identities of their own lives.

Dreams provide a useful bridge between the immediacy of play-acting and the expanded perspective of narration. Jessie, Lena's older sister, became more controlled as she grew older, less drawn to the consciously magical. For her, dreams transformed situations. Her conflicts often concerned struggles between girls and boys. One of these she recorded at the age of six:

When I was at school, a boy was chasing me. Then he tripped me. And before I knew it, I was in another world. And the boy was a baby. We were back in time!!!!!!! It looked like we were in space. There were so many different shapes!!! And I had to be the boy's mother!! And me and the baby lived happily ever after.

When I asked her to illustrate the dream, she drew a large whale shape floating in space among various winding shapes. The whale had eyes, nose and mouth and a door in its side. Inside was a woman labeled "Mama" holding a baby. Also inside was an elephant's head.

This dream, even though it went back into the past, allowed her to envision a future where she will be powerful. Another dream, recorded about a year later (after her own mother decided to go back to school), imagined another powerful option for transforming fear into success:

I got into the refrigerator because I thought if I ate something, it would calm me down and I wouldn't have a monster dream like I had the night before. So in my dream we had a whole bunch of food, it was a magic refrigerator. It was like Alice in Wonderland. The refrigerator had a hole in the door I could crawl through. At first it was tiny and then I put my finger in and it started growing. Inside the door there was a whole bunch of other doors, like stained glass, and then I picked one of the doors, it was a weird shape, it was shaped sort of round, like the hole, all the doors were shaped like that, and when I got in there, it was like a room with a whole bunch of switches and then a whole bunch of other people started coming out because there was a whole bunch of noise coming from the radio that you had to switch to turn it on. And I found out it was a college for boys. I could tell there was a whole bunch of books, everybody carried books around and they're weren't any girls except for me and everybody was big, including me. Then as soon as we were about to have a big party, I woke up.

The continuity of narrative served a healing as well as a growth function for Jennifer and Dan, sister and brother. Their growing up was marked by trauma. Dan is the second son. Two children born after him, Eric and Erika, both died of a lingering and disabling brain disease before the age of four. Jennifer, who was born last, was carefully monitored by anxious parents until she was out of danger, and then treated like a miracle child.

Dan's problems came out in school where, due partially to eye problems, his work was sloppy. After a teacher in public school kept picking on him, his mother switched him to a Catholic school. A sensitive, relational and very imaginative child, he flourished with certain teachers and withered with others. One year when he wasn't doing so well, I offered to tutor him. To ease the stress of schoolwork, I first took him through a deep relaxation. To my surprise he went immediately into an obviously familiar trance state. Afterwards he told me about his psychic experiences. Instead of doing math we had a fascinating discussion of other worlds and where spirits go when people die.

His interest in planets and time/space dimensions led to a fascination with science, particularly astronomy and electronics. Recently, he went back to public school and won a second prize at the science fair for a project which created a natural environment. This showed me how an intuitive child can channel his curiosity into exploring nature. For him there really is no contradiction between the magic of his imagination and the magic of the world out there.

But before all that could happen, he had to do some healing, particularly in relation to the fear and grief engendered by his early childhood experience of watching both brother and sister slowly die. This healing came partially in the form of stories he told, which I encouraged him to write down and, in some cases, illustrate. Here is a story he wrote when he was six:

Buster the Bunny

Buster the bunny was going to sail across the sea on his boat. About 400 years ago Sparkle his brother sailed across the sea and never returned to the island. Many bunnies said he made it to America. Others say his ship was sunk in a storm but nobody knows and Buster was going to find out. His parents did not want him to go, but he was going to go anyway. He started early in the morning. Buster sailed for 14 days and 14 nights. On the 15th day a big storm came! The sail tore in half, the waves were higher than the boat, he hit a rock and it made a hole in the side of the boat, and he crashed on the coast of Virginia.

Jennifer, his sister, discovered her healing energy through an identification with horses. Ever since she was little, she acted out the rainbow pony. The story she told was about isolation, perhaps as the only survivor of the last three children, perhaps as the only girl, perhaps as a result of being both pampered and resented:

> One day there was a horse and he had no friends so he had to look for one. So he was walking a long distance and he got tired and tired. So there was a pond near by and he took a drink of water and he saw a little bear across the stream. So he stopped to talk to him. Then he went on and on. And he found a little broken boat. And he knew that somebody was nearby. And he could find some food. So he walked fast and found a little house. And somebody took him in and kept him for her horse. It was a girl and her name was Jessie.

These stories and dreams reveal the connecting lines each child had to create to give continuity to, as well as allow change in, her or his life. Jessie needed to imagine herself as powerful in order to deal with her daily struggles with boys. Dan needed, imaginatively, to go through the danger his siblings had suffered in order to allow himself to be a survivor. Jennifer needed to identify with horses in order to tap into energy for exploring the world on her own.

I am also fascinated with stories the children have created together. The following dialogue is a sample from when the Heart Gang went to the local playground:

> "The sea monster is going to take over this playground if we don't get this ship going. C'mon."
> "Wait'll I get off this boat, Jessie."
> "I'm not Jessie."
> "Yeah, I know, you're Jem." (Fictional character)
> "Sisters, I'm sinking; help me."
> "I'm gonna close my eyes so if someone gets hurt, it won't be my fault."
> "We're the rescuers."
> "She's the bad guy."
> "No, I'm your sister."
> "Your sister's the bad guy."
> "The bad guy, help!"
> "I'm commanding this ship."

"She's meaner than she looks."
"Can't you be mean back?"
"But she's my sister."

The play here is not at the service of plot continuity. The focus is on the dynamics between the players: who can suggest the most compelling script, who gets to be the hero, who's IT (the bad guy), who feels left out, how real roles (sisters) impinge on pretend roles, who calls the rules ("Last one out is a rotten egg," for example) and so on.

But there were times, perhaps induced by this more structure-conscious adult, when they agreed on or created together a more consistent story line, starting again with who:

"I'm the unicorn."
"I'm the little girl that's lost in the woods."
"I'm the princess."

As soon as I, the narrator, began with "Once upon a time," I was interrupted by "Wait, we're not ready yet," and then an explanation of what I should say.

"You have to say, 'Once upon a time, there was a king, two daughters, and a princess and a unicorn.'"

This was followed by more discussion of possible characters (the poor old lady) and plot twists (the poor little girl is a princess in disguise because everybody's trying to steal her magic; the unicorn has fallen out of the clouds).

"And I helped you and took care of you."
"No, I found you."
"No, I helped her because she took a walk in the woods."
"I wanna find you, please!"
Then as narrator, I asked: "Do we have all our pieces now?"
"No."
"We all tell our part."
"We're going to start with the poor little girl."
"She has to dress up." (Sounds of costuming)
"Jennifer, pretend I transformed into a little girl."
"You two aren't in Act I. First I save you and then we both save her."

Act I

King (Jessie, singing): I wonder, I wonder if my daughter will return.
Narrator (me): Once upon a time there was a king, there was a princess, there was a unicorn who came down from the sky, and there was a princess who disguised herself, and we'll let her tell you about her disguise.
Poor Little Girl (Lena): Once when I was growing up, I was scared of my powers, I did not know what they were, and then I noticed I was different from all the other babies. I was green and then when I started growing older, I started to be pink and then yellow and then peach, and then my hair turned green, peach, red, brown and finally yellow. Once I was seven I noticed that I had powers and magic: when I pushed a boy, he flew all the way to Mars. I did not know how it happened, but a kid came up and told me I had magic powers, and everybody wanted to have them.

(Clapping from the other actors: a polite way of ending Lena's monologue, followed by a decisive announcement from Jessie: "Act II. Characters in Act II please report to duty and costumes.")

Act II

Unicorn (Jennifer): Once upon a time there was a unicorn who came out of the sky and fell into a trap, and then a princess who was walking through the woods found me and helped me. (Sounds of a neighing horse.)
Princess (Jessie): Pretend one of your legs is hurt and I bandage you and from then on I take care of you until the leg is healed and from then on we were partners. And one day we were riding through the woods, and I noticed that my sister hadn't been home for a long time. The unicorn went into the water. (Sounds of water splashing) She said "I'm thirsty, I need some water." (The princess here also spoke for or translated for the unicorn who made only horse sounds.) And we continued our walk. But one day we saw...
Little Girl: ...a little girl, a poor little girl.
Princess: The princess in disguise. And when we found her, she was stuck in a net. And I said "Who are you, little one?"

Little Girl: Who are you?
Princess: I am Princess Lillian.
Little Girl: Princess, princess, I am your sister.
Princess: Are you trapped in this net? Oh yes, and this is my unicorn.
Little Girl: I didn't want anyone to have my powers because they would take them away from me. But they wanted my sister's powers because hers are much stronger than mine.
Princess: Mine go much deeper. I have much, much more power. I can turn a leaf into dust.
Unicorn: And I, the unicorn have most power of all, I can turn anything into whatever I want, like an elephant. I can turn into a piece of leaf in a second. And I can fly and make magical powers with a cloud in danger.
(A conflict develops over whose powers are strongest.)
King (smoking his pipe): My daughters, do not fight. Do not fight.
Little Girl (to the others): You will turn everything into dust. You will make everything miserable in your life. You will make everything that you do bad. You will not ever, ever get married.
Unicorn: I will never allow any people to come to my world, Unicornland.
Princess: If one person enters Unicornland, they will be killed.
Unicorn: The people will kill all the unicorns, for meat and horns. There was a spell put on the unicorn world by an old witch who was mean. Any unicorn who is not a baby who leaves the unicorn land will be killed.
Narrator: I am the good witch. I want to take away the spell, but I can't do it by myself. I want help.
All three: We'll help you.
Narrator: I need all your powers. What is your power? How are you going to help?
King/Princess: I can turn all evil into good.
Little Girl: I will turn everything into beauty and forgiveness.
Unicorn: Everything will be at peace and happiness. And no one will fight. They will get along good together and have a good time, and so on and so on, and the world will last forever. (Neighing)
Little Girl: Unicorn, please forgive us. I will give you back this horn so you will have more power in the world than anyone.

We have been selfish.
Unicorn: Yes, I will forgive you.
Princess: Forgive only the people where happiness will be.
Little Girl: Well, then, we must return the unicorn.
Princess: You cannot go, you'll be killed. Everyone, give me the power and I will change it.
Little Girl: I cannot give you the power. I am going to turn into a unicorn. I have a tiny bit left to turn into anything I want.
Unicorn: What about the witch?
Princess: I know the witch and she is very evil. I know her castle, deep in the mountains that separate people.
Unicorn: I'll never go there. Did you know that all of the unicorns have been trapped there?
Princess: I've been there. I tried to get away. Luckily I did. I noticed all the unicorns' horns and that everything had been killed.
Unicorn: And there is a beast that comes out at night and traps all the unicorns that are running wild. He is made of fire, he is a bull, he takes them into the water and when the waves come, you can see the unicorns' horns and faces, oh, they are tired of being trapped in that pool underground. Wicked witch!
Little Girl: And they turn into mermaids.
Princess: And they never get out. And I'm the only one who can change them back.
Unicorn: You're not the only one. (Another scuffle about who has the most power.)
Narrator: Together.
Unicorn: Together we can all do it, we can change the evil witch.
Little Girl: Break!

And that was the end of that story.

Despite my attempts to steer the plot toward the more politically-correct (cooperation, good witches), the power of pre-established story lines and of the girls' own psychic projections pulled them back toward the evil witch and their battles over control. Cooperation is appealing after you have experienced your own individual power. Power can't be shared until it is claimed.

Despite my attempts to record a coherent play, the real energy for the girls did not come from producing a product. It came when they actually dropped into their characters and started playing out the dangerous, and inherited, context they had established. Although they listened to the tape, the story itself evaporated as a bond between them. Next time they played together, the story was different.

This evanescence is not true of the saga which Dan and his friend Richard created together. Although they may have privately enacted a process similar to the one above, what they presented to me was a story with a life of its own, complete with its own cosmology, generations of characters and interwoven plot sequences. A Russian novel couldn't be more complex. They have been creating this story together for the past five years, ever since they were in the second grade together. I was the first adult with whom the story had been shared.

The boys started with play-acting:

Richard: On Planet Zero, the crystal castle is being sieged by the dreaded light entities. We join our heroes in their battle. (Then follows a sequence of weapon sounds.)
Richard: Dan, they're taking over the castle, what are we going to do?
Dan: Shoot up the photon beams and put on the cloaking devices.
Richard: How about you calling the rest of the army? (A highly elaborate series of sounds follows.)
Richard: It's not doing that much good. Let's fall back and get our plans together. Fall back. (More weapon sounds)
Richard: Uh oh, I think that was the wrong decision to make, *Dan*. They just took over the castle.
Dan: Okay, report to all stations: Retreat, repeat, retreat; we are evacuating from Planet Zero to Planet X. This is not a drill. All stations: retreat. I'm going to the ship room to make sure everything turns out all right. (More weapon sounds)
Richard: (A sound of somebody getting hit): Ahhhhg.
Dan: Richard!
Richard: That wasn't me! (More sounds of weapons)
Richard: See ya.
Dan: You two—forty-two and sixty-eight. Get the minor photon ships. Join in the battle. Twenty-four and thirty-one, come with me. (Weapon sounds)
Dan: Okay, charge the engines. Is the matrix on? ("Matrix on, sir.") Okay, energize. (Vehicle sounds: "We are leaving Planet Zero, sir.")

Richard as a Light Being: Aha, I've finally conquered this worthless planet. What do you have to say about that, Master?
Dan as Master: Very good. Now we will start for Planet X. They will have their main fields open. We must penetrate the fields. The Master has spoken. (Then follows a strategy discussion between the two heroes which ends with):
Richard: As leaders, I guess we have to lead it. In the front.
Dan: Of course. I'll take 642 guards; you'll take 643 guards.
Richard: Why do I have one more than you do?
Dan: Because one died, remember?
Richard: Oh, I guess the rest of them lived.
Dan: Okay, you guys come with me. (More weapon sounds)
Richard: Don't tell me they're attacking this planet too. (Elaborate weapon sounds)
Richard: Where the heck are you? I can't see nothing.
Dan: It's too cloudy. They must be using smoke bombs.
Richard: No, I think they're using super tear gas. (Coughing)
Dan: I'm going into the second dimension. That way no one can touch us.
Richard: I'll go into the zero (coughing), get a couple of weapons I left behind there, which might help us.
Dan: Turn off the matrix, we're entering the second dimension. (More weapon sounds)
Richard: I'll need this, and this, that and that. Put on this smoke mask. (More weapon sounds. Coughing)
Dan: Okay, guys, stop firing. ("We're going down, sir, we've been hit." Sounds of crash)
Richard: Dan, you okay?
Dan: Yeah, I'm fine. I can't say that for the barracks though. (Weapons sounds)
Richard: Uh oh, I think we're in trouble.
Dan: Okay, now we're evacuating Planet X. Go into the crystal castle. (Weapon sounds)
Richard: We don't have a choice, the master light entity's here. (Weapon sounds) Dan, remember those special powers that we got from the future, that we promised we wouldn't use?
Dan: Yeah, I think it's time to use them. (Weapon sounds)
Richard: Just send them back.
Dan: Ready? Summon our powers. (Sounds)
Richard: Fire! (Sounds) We still got the rest of the army.

Dan: Okay, I'm going to use every piece of power in my body. (Sounds of weapons)
Richard: Well, we got rid of them for now, I hope, unless they have traps around here. Let's go clean up the ones on Planet Zero. (End of this part of the story.)

Because of my own gender bias, I find the twists and turns in the girls' stories more intriguing than the victories and defeats of the boys. I am even less enchanted with the various weapon systems. But I was impressed with the variety and precision of the sounds they made—lasers, rockets, bombs, zapps. Each had its own distinct pitch, resonance and sequence. The sounds were like musical improvisation. Had the boys been playing instruments instead of shooting weapons, they would have been creating jazz. Noise is a way of having impact on the environment. Unfortunately, boys are generally socialized to channel that power into weapons of destruction rather than tools for harmony.

After this playacting, the boys went on for another two hours to tell me the whole Super Ninja story. The sources for their plots were no more original than the girls'. They had chosen elements from popular culture and synthesized them into their own alternative world. They were careful to point out where their version differed from the original. In the process of developing the drama, they were dealing with any number of personal issues and empowering themselves (albeit, alas, in gender-stereotypic roles). Both Dan and Richard are loners, outsiders at school. Richard's father is blind and relies on Richard for help. Neither boy is particularly athletic or aggressive. For both potency comes through imagination.

In their script, they play creatures who are half-Ninja (hairy creature with phenomenal powers and longevity) and half-human. The boys choose distinct characters (Dan is a scientist and Richard is a warrior), but the personalities and names are pretty much their own.

The story spans the ultimates in time and space:

Richard: In the beginning at the time when earth is being created, Planet Zero was under a very big attack by Sharkman and his evil force controlled by the overall master, Prime.
Dan: There were two young princes and one princess. The only thing was to evacuate them to earth because they would

be the soldiers of the future and would rule the galaxy as they grew older.
Richard: They were sent there and, on their way out, they saw their father, and they do have good memories, being stabbed through the neck with a sword by Prime.
Dan: Which destroyed the Super Ninja.
Richard: That is its only weakness, the neck.

Fortunately for the future, not all of their adventures are battles. In one scene they rescue a poor planet by buying seeds from the few wealthy landowners, which they then give to the poor people to plant so they can grow their own food. A bloodless revolution.

Their story includes several generations, many centuries, multiple dimensions (black holes, white holes, red holes) and zones, technologies and breeds (kinds of Ninjas), governments, hierarchies and roles, a number of planets and galaxies and a host of heroes and villains, life forms and psychic powers. It draws inspiration from those blurry areas where science and theology, politics and magic mix. They have mapped and plotted this world as if it were real. As they told it, they alternated, without conflict and with little disagreement, the role of narrator.

I was not only honored to be privy to this heretofore private creation but impressed by its complexity. These were stories they had worked out, acted out and agreed upon over a five year period (almost half of their lives). While the whole saga is too long to tell here, and also not mine to tell, here is a sample of some of the issues negotiated within the text:

Richard: We were killed once, but every time we got killed we were on Planet Zero, and Planet Zero has a strange effect on Super Ninjas. As it sucks the soul as it's leaving the body, it gives the body time to rest till the soul goes back up into the body and there is no harm done. Which is why we have been able to die and be re-erected so many times, about forty.
Dan: Super Ninjas live for hundreds of billions of centuries. The normal life span of a Super Ninja is over sixty-one-quadrillion years.

Several weeks after we recorded the tale, the boys told me that they were celebrating the fifth anniversary of their storytelling. They shared with me an account of its origin and their contingency plan for getting in touch with each other if they were ever separated. Clearly they recognized how their shared creation was a crucial bond between them. Even though they had some vague plans about marketing their creation, their central concern, with a keen awareness of change over centuries, was that the relationship between them continue.

The difference between the stories of the boys and the girls is not only a difference of gender, although that certainly provides a striking contrast. Age and the need as we get older to have the continuity and consistency that a more coherent story provides also contributed to the difference. The girls were six, seven and eight when they recorded their play. The boys were twelve when they told their story. Also, the boys have experienced separation, when Dan changed schools, and they live in different neighborhoods, whereas the girls are sisters and close neighbors, so for the boys the story itself is the primary bond.

Gender differences come out in content, roles, plots and conflicts. Although both like to rescue people and both have power issues, the heroism of the girls predictably depends on healing while the heroism of the boys depends on survival and victory (killing). In the playacting stage, although both can drop into a variety of people roles, the boys tend also to drop into machines (vehicles, weapons) while the girls tend to drop into animals (a favorite being horses).

Developmentally, within a linear model, intuition is considered part of the "magical thinking" stage. As children grow up, psychologists warn that this stage must be discarded for more rational processes. The association of intuition with childhood, therefore, becomes one more reason to dismiss intuition as childish. I, however, offer the experience of children as an opportunity to learn again what we adults have usually forgotten.

Within an alternative developmental model, more in tune with wholistic perception, we grow by cumulative layers, with each new ring enhancing rather than replacing another. We don't stop walking once we've learned to talk or talking once we've learned to read. Scientific inquiry shouldn't have to eliminate a belief in symbol and myth. Examples from nature suggest that what is acquired first is often most essential for survival, not the least important. Trees, despite their adaptability to changing conditions of sun, rain and wind, depend on a primary root system and a healthy core if they are to survive. The fact that intuition can be like child's play does not make it obsolete as we grow older.

Because children trust intuitive language, it serves many purposes for them: a way of learning her/history; a way of personal growth, self-expression and empowerment; a way of healing; a way of remembering and giving continuity to various experiences; a way of explaining mysteries; a process of connecting; and a way to create a product which bonds. Intuitive language is no less powerful for us adults, if we are willing to learn what the children have to show us.

Many of us complain about the passivity of children in front of TV. But these children seem to me more actively and creatively engaged with the myths of our world than many adult consumers of mass culture. We can't blame them if the values those myths convey are less than ideal. If more of us were actively engaged in telling the stories, perhaps those values could change.

CHAPTER SIX

Symbolic Transformation

INTUITIVE, OR symbolic language, being both concrete and inclusive, thrives on the challenge of unifying multiple facets. But it's no freer than discursive language of dominating absolutes. These must be wrestled with, as if they were angels. They must be pinned to the ground, disrobed of their distancing and falsely universalizing splendor, and forced to walk along with us down unmarked trails.

When a person reaches for an image to express an intuitive realization, her tendency is to search through a store of images traditionally used in the language of intuition. The danger is that, however fresh the vision, the expression will be through images so overused, trite or stereotyped that the energy has drained from them. When expressed in such worn-out language, the communication goes flat.

Another even greater danger is the misuse of common, still powerful symbols. Certain images are so charged with meaning for whole groups that they have become cultural symbols. Examples are the medicine wheel, the tree of life, the cross, the spiral, the yin/yang, the *nkisi*. And some images or symbols, and their accompanying narratives, occur in more than one culture: the sacred twins, the pregnant virgin, the dead god or goddess, the serpent, the divine bird, exile in the desert.

Jung called such symbols, and the impulses behind them, archetypes; the feminist literary critic Rachel Duplessis calls them prototypes; James Hillman considers them "the deepest patterns of psychic functioning" (23); and Joseph Campbell, in his work on mythology, universalizes them. There is considerable debate about how universal they are, given varied cultures' different interpretations of the same symbol or impulse. Observe how evil the snake is in some traditions, notably Christian, and how sacred in others, the Dahomean rainbow serpent, for example.

Whether or not they are universal, there is no doubt such symbols are powerful. Used for the wrong reasons they can become tools to manipulate people. When attached to certain fixed meanings, they can be as dangerous as weapons. Consider the Nazi abuse of the ancient symbol of the swastika or the KKK's use of the burning cross to perpetuate racism. Because of its feminine/masculine duality the yin/yang symbol has reenforced gender stereotypes. And the symbolism of the chakras can be used to reinforce a caste system. The fault is not in the symbols themselves but in the consciousness which employs them to express contradictory values. The problem is that by depicting such symbols we can perpetuate a value system we didn't mean to articulate. Thus the girls and their evil witches, the boys and their destructive heroes.

For these reasons, we must wrestle with these absolutising symbols so they don't continue to dominate our intuitive language. In this chapter I look at narratives by contemporary women writers Maxine Hong Kingston, Ursula LeGuin and Doris Lessing which struggle with the archetypes of yin/yang and the chakra system and transform them so they are no longer sexist or classist. To do this, they must take symbols

Yin/Yang

which are fixed, like statues, in meanings which negate or devalue the experience of many people within the cultures they embody and bring them to life again. The symbols help unify their tales while their tales vitalize and change the symbols.

The narratives I'm looking at are LeGuin's *The Left Hand of Darkness*, Kingston's *Woman Warrior*, Lessing's *The Marriages Between Zones Three, Four and Five*. In each, the unifying symbols give structure and continuity to the stories, while the stories give life, movement, relevance, and transformative power to the symbols.

When these women wrestle with such archetypes, infusing them with a new dynamism, they transform them to uses more in keeping with feminist visions of wholeness. Each of the works here expresses a primary fragmentation which causes suffering for whole societies, as well as a vision by which this split can be healed or transformed.

These symbols serve as structural principles because their meanings expand into multiple dimensions, simultaneously describing a person as well as the world s/he lives in, a moment as well as an overall pattern of movement. For both LeGuin and Kingston the structuring symbol is the yin/yang.

For Lessing the structuring symbol is suggested by the concept of Zones in her title. These zones not only mark the boundaries between different countries in her book, but also suggest the energy centers or chakra points of a single body.

The yin/yang or Tai Chi symbol represents the unity of the two primary energies of the universe. They are polar opposites and complementary. Each contains the seed of the other. They are constantly changing and transforming into each other, and cannot exist apart from each other. Yang is the active principle and yin is the passive one, but both arise from Tao, which is the original undivided oneness or ultimate nothingness. For mystics this primal essence manifests either as all-is-one or as the void. In western terms, yang is energy and yin is form. The *I Ching*, or *Book of Changes*, describes all the possible combinations and transformations of yin/yang, sixty-four in all, starting with number one, the pure yang energy—the Creative, and number two, the pure yin energy—the Receptive. Other aspects of this polarization of energies, according to tradition, are:

YIN	YANG
earth	heaven
moon	sun
things female	things male
inside	outside
night	day
the right side	the left side
the front of the body	the back of the body
conservation	destruction
responsiveness	aggression
contraction	expansion
cold	hot

(Hua-Ching, 18)

The Left Hand of Darkness

What signals LeGuin's use of the yin/yang symbol is her title, *The Left Hand of Darkness*. The symbol itself is revealed during the bonding at the heart of this book. Estraven, the exiled native, shares with his companion, Genly Ai, the emissary from other worlds, Tormer's Lay:

> Light is the left hand of darkness
> and darkness the right hand of light.
> Two are one, life and death, lying
> together like lovers in kemmer,
> like hands joined together,
> like the end and the way (233).

At this point Ai, unable to respond fully, suggests that Estraven, "isolated and undivided," is "as obsessed with wholeness as we are with dualism," and Estraven responds that "duality is an essential...so long as there is myself and the other" (234).

Later, Ai makes a connection between this song and the Tai Chi symbol, but only after he realizes the love between himself and Estraven:

> It was from the difference between us, not from the affinities and likenesses, but from the difference, that love came; and it was itself the bridge, the only bridge, across what divided us (249).

Then Ai drew "the double curve within the circle and blacked the yin half of the symbol," which he showed to Estraven, who did not recognize it:

> It is yin and yang. "Light is the left hand of darkness"... Light, dark. Fear, courage. Cold, warmth. Female, male. It is yourself... Both and one. A shadow on snow (267).

This symbol of the balancing of opposites is key to this story of bonding between two persons and the worlds they represent. Both persons are aliens. Estraven Harth (estranged from the hearth) is separated from his home because of incest, separated from his country because of treachery. Genly Ai ("his name a cry of pain,") is cut off from his family, who are growing old and dying as he travels through space/time, and out of touch with his feminine side, his shadow. While Ai is a divided person from a united world, Estraven is a whole person trapped in a divided world.

This apparently science fiction novel is not prescriptive of a future, possibly ideal world. It's a symbolic description of our world, divided at the time of writing (published in 1969) into East and West and split along gender lines. The ice in the novel, in the world of Winter, along with the focus on borders, speaks of the cold war as well as divided selves.

Before there can be communal bonding across these boundaries, personal bonding must take place:

> Not We and They; not I and It; but I and Thou. Not political, not pragmatic, but mystical (259).

Neither the West, Karhide with its hierarchies, individual egos and passions, nor Orgoreyn with its collective order and colorless passivity can provide the setting for this transformation. It must take place at the "heart of warmth" in the solitude of the ice. Before personal bonding can take place, there must be a healing of energies within each person. As long as the microcosm is wounded, the macrocosm cannot be healed. Nor can a fully healed microcosm survive within a diseased macrocosm.

For Genly Ai this healing requires an integration of his feminine side. Although from a wise world, he is internally alienated by his own misogyny and homophobia, cut off from his own left hand of darkness, the sinister, the feminine. The inhabitants of Gethen are both androgynous and bisexual, but he describes all their negative traits in feminine terms: "They behaved like animals in that respect, or like women"(49).

Estraven to him at first was "womanly, all charm and tact and lack of substance" (12). His stereotyping of the feminine as devious, bland, faithless, prying, spying and bovine leads to his mistrust of Estraven, the only person on either side of this world who understands his mission and who is capable of bringing it to fruition. As the missionary he is the seed without soil, the sperm without an egg.

He begins to understand the power of yin energy in the presence of the Handara, a mystical community practicing a kind of zen or tao, without priests, hierarchy, vows or creed. These people find their healing power and visions through an "untrance" involving self-loss and extreme sensual receptiveness. Faxe the Weaver, a natural empath, at the height of her/his power and receptivity, clearly manifests as a woman. But Ai keeps this experience at a distance by labeling it "stagnant, ignorant" (60).

Ai's healing comes from a yielding of his excessively yang energy to the yin energy which shadows him in the person of Estraven (Estrogen?). This can happen only after he has been arrested and stripped down to the emptiness of the yin state, forced into imprisonment and passive suffering: the seed broken open. Even after he is rescued by Estraven and is wrapped up on the sled as if dead, he cannot fully accept this other side:

> There was in this attitude something feminine, a refusal of the abstract, the ideal, a submissiveness to the given,
> which rather displeased me (212).

Even when they exchange first names, Genly refuses to trust Estraven fully: "What is a friend in a world where any friend may be a lover at a new phase of the moon?" Eventually, though still patronizing Estraven as "built more like a woman than a man, more fat than muscle," (218), he recognizes that Estraven is free from male ego and confesses that in his own world, "the heaviest single factor in one's life" is whether one is born male or female (234).

His healing occurs only when he admits and accepts the difference between them, the fact that Estraven is a woman as well as a man. This fact he is forced to see when Estraven goes into kemmer, a state of sexual excitement where one temporarily displays a specific sex, and with it, a more unified gender.

Only then could they share mindspeech. Only then could Ai rescue Estraven from falling into the blue crevice. Only then as an affirmation of Estraven's wholeness did Ai draw the symbol of the tai chi: "female/male, it is yourself, Therem, both and one."

While Ai is shadowed by Estraven, Estraven is shadowed by his brother/sibling who was his lover, whose suicide led to Estraven's exile from his home. While Ai is threatened by difference, Estraven is threatened by sameness. His own family banishes him; his own country calls him a traitor. Haunted by guilt and regret over a life "which lay behind me like a broken promise," he is healed by the promise of a future which can expand beyond the narrow, restrictive roles within family dynamics and political intrigues.

For Estraven the bonding with Ai provides a mirroring of his own isolation. Empathizing with Ai's frailty on the ice, he asks why Ai was sent to this world alone and vulnerable.

> Alone I cannot change your world. But I can be changed by it. Alone, I must listen, as well as speak (259).

Here Ai is expressing his own transformation as well as articulating a clue to Estraven's own transformation.

> Up here on the ice each of us is singular, isolate, I as cut off from those like me, from my society and its rulers, as he from his, we are equals at last, equal, alien, alone.

With this realization Estraven is able to affirm his/her own wholeness. In so doing he heals the wound caused by his brother's death. Hearing his brother's voice in the telepathic communication between himself and Ai, he finds in this non-sexual bond between strangers a friendship which actualizes a more expansive identity.

Estraven moves from constrictions of shifgrethor, or shadow, to love. From the demands of personal pride, ego, honor, prestige, "face," patriotism, he moves through accusations, misunderstandings and false impressions to a bonding across great differences. He can do this because he has the intuition of the larger unity, the larger whole which Ai's arrival promises. He has "the power of seeing, if only for a flash, everything at once; seeing whole" (204).

While Ai's yang energy is balanced by contraction toward that ultimate emptiness deeper than the arrogance of ego, Estraven's yin energy is healed by expansion beyond the cutting icy edges of the shells of home and country which he has outgrown.

The book structures the interplay of the yin/yang energies through alternating perspectives, Ai's notes and Estraven's journal, as well as balancing perspectives. The female investigator's notes, for instance, give a more positive, less sexist interpretation to the Gethenian ambisexuality than do Ai's. The ancient myths give depth and resonance to the roots of Estraven's world.

While some of the sexist language (even the androgynous Estraven uses the generic "he" and the universal "man") is bothersome, this book, written on the eve of the rebirth of the women's movement, is a brilliant example of LeGuin's intuitive ability to see what energies in our society are split, out of balance, in need of healing. Her novel exemplifies the "foretelling" of both contemporary feminism and the recent dismantling of the wall between east and west. It does so through "farfetching": "the intuitive perception of a moral entity" which "tends to find expression not in rational symbols but in metaphor" (147).

Woman Warrior

The yin/yang symbol is just as central in Kingston's *Woman Warrior*, but it is not as explicitly stated. It's taken for granted, a part of her cultural heritage as mundane as her mother's concern over whether she ate too much yin food (117).

While Kingston also explores issues of sexism and xenophobia, she is especially tuned to the natural order of shifting energies. She focuses on those points of development where yin produces yang and yang produces yin.

The key description of the integration of yin/yang energies comes during her shamanic training:

> I saw two people made of gold dancing the earth's dances. They turned so perfectly that together they were the axis of the earth's turning (32).

This manifestation was universal: Chinese, African, Javanese, Hindu, American Indian.

In the language of metaphor with which Kingston is so articulate, this dance describes the yin/yang principle, both fixed and spinning. As part of her vision quest, this vision opens a "small crack in the mystery" (33) which she ponders throughout the rest of the book. While this passage shows her respect for this ancient wisdom, part of what she does in this autobiography is challenge its patriarchal application: yin is "all things female" while yang is "all things male."

The movement of the book, although it spans several centuries and the Pacific Ocean, is primarily within Kingston's mind. It begins with the story her mother tells her not to tell and ends with a story in her own voice. The shift in her energies from yin to yang is supported by the structure of the book. By alternating between yin and yang, the book as a whole explores how to balance those energies.

The first story, "No Name Woman," is about her aunt who shamed the family by killing herself. She was punished for having a girl baby outside of marriage in hard times when food was scarce and there were already too many mouths to feed. The story is as much about

Maxine's speculations, circling round and round the meager facts, as it is about the aunt condemned to oblivion simply because she was born a woman. Although intended by her mother as a cautionary tale about sex, it becomes for Maxine an example of excessive yin energy:

> The heavy, deep-rooted women were to maintain the past against the flood, safe for [the men's] returning.... So my aunt crossed boundaries not delineated in space (9).

Just as Estraven suffered from the constrictions of yin energy in his country, so No Name Woman is punished by the villagers, her neighbors. They intend:

> to show her a personal, physical representation of the break she had made in the "roundness"...[of their communal life] (14).

By disregarding the constriction of the yin pattern upon women, she had broken out of the circle the yin/yang symbol makes as a whole. "This roundness had to be made coin-sized so that she would see its circumference" (15). For a woman the circle is not a flexible polarity but a single, inexorable fate, the side of preservation and stasis.

No wonder Maxine is haunted by this woman. "My mother said we were lucky we didn't have to have our feet bound when we were seven" (11). But she's still caught in a double bind. By remaining silent (not even asking her aunt's name) Maxine participates in the family's punishment of forgetting, in a tradition known for honoring ancestors. In so doing she accepts the patriarchal judgment. If she tells on her, takes her own step beyond those boundaries, her aunt's ghost might pull Maxine down into the well with her.

Just as yin and yang each contain the seed of the other, so this excess of yin energy turns into yang energy in the next story, "White Tigers." Here Maxine integrates into her consciousness the stories of women warriors. She points out the contradiction that even though Chinese girls are destined to be wives or slaves, there is a tradition in the old stories of heroines, swordswomen. "Perhaps women were once so dangerous that they had to have their feet bound" (23).

Not only are these stories about powerful women, they reveal the power of the story teller, Maxine's mother. In making the story her own, identifying as the heroine, Maxine empowers herself as storyteller as well as warrior.

In the story she becomes the little girl who at seven leaves the constrictions of family and village and follows a bird into the mountains to meet an old woman and man (the yin and yang). They give her the traditional training of a shaman/warrior: learning how to be silent, how to move in circles, how to imitate the animals, how to survive. When her self-discipline is sufficiently developed, she goes on a solitary quest. Fasting leads to a vision of the archetypal yin/yang dancers.

For another eight years the old people train her "in dragon ways," the ability to see the whole of life's energies, the Tao: "You have to infer the whole dragon from the parts you can see and touch" (34). As a result, she learns "to make my mind large, as the universe is large, so that there is room for paradoxes."

Finally she is ready as a warrior to return to her village. Even though married, she has a baby between battles, she keeps the fact that she is a woman hidden. After leading a revolution and installing a new emperor, she goes home as a "female avenger" to kill the baron who had wronged her family, the tyrant who tried to appeal to her "man to man" by quoting the all-too-familiar sayings: "Girls are maggots in the rice"; "It is more profitable to raise geese than daughters" (50).

After such a glorious fantasy, returning to the yin reality of her actual life is almost intolerable. Not only is there the inherited sexism to deal with but also the repressive "American feminine" model. Caught in the double-bind between being a good girl (slave) and a bad girl (almost as good as being a boy), caught in the gap between old world and new, she both bemoans her powerlessness and takes energy from identification with the warrior woman, with whom she shares the suffering of words *sexist*, *racist* carved into her back.

In the third and middle story, "Shaman," we find a balance of yin and yang energies in one person, a real woman, Maxine's mother. Her power is not just talking-story but living it.

This story tells of her training and life as a doctor in China. Not only is she brilliant in studying the ways of the new medicine, she is courageous in handling the old ghosts. She proves herself capable of healing psychic as well as physical disease. She is as much at home in the yin dimension as she is in the yang; she can take in as well as give out. She is the Dragon, the Tao, the wholeness which contains both yin and yang energies. When at the end of this story she calls Maxine

"Little Dog" ("a name to fool the gods"), Maxine knows "I am really a Dragon, as she is a Dragon" (127).

But with aging and immigration, Maxine's mother, Brave Orchid, loses her power. Although she gives birth to six children after the age of forty-five, in America she is no longer able to practice medicine. Instead she is forced to spend long hours laboring in the family laundry. The fourth story, "In the Western Palace," records the moment when her yang power turns to yin.

When her sister Moon Orchid comes to America, Brave Orchid attempts to reconcile her with her husband, now a wealthy doctor. He left her in China years ago and has remarried. Unfortunately in the process Moon Orchard goes crazy and eventually must be institutionalized. The futility of this effort and its disastrous effects on Moon Orchid spell out, in poignant detail, the loss of Brave Orchid's power. The dragon has been defeated by age and the American way. But this is not treated as a tragedy. It is considered part of a natural cycle, falling from ripeness.

The next stage of this cycle of transformation belongs to Maxine, no longer in fantasy but in reality. In the final story, "A Song for A Barbarian Reed Pipe," we see how she claims the latent dragon power for herself. To do so she breaks out of her own silence, her entrapment in the yin role designed for women. First blaming her silence on her mother for cutting her tongue, she then realizes it is a product of having to speak a foreign language, English, at school, and of adapting to American sound patterns requiring women to whisper to be feminine.

To ease her own silence, she attacks another Chinese girl even more silent than she is, projecting her self-hatred and vulnerability onto this victim. But she can't make the girl talk. Defeated by this yin energy as well as her own guilt, she develops a mysterious illness and spends the next eighteen months in solitary yin.

Then, afraid of going crazy and terrified of an arranged marriage, Maxine quacks through her "pressed duck" voice to tell her mother a list of things piling up inside her head so she won't feel so alone with them. But her mother is too busy to listen.

Finally "my throat burst open. I stood up, talking and burbling." She stands up to her mother about being married off, about the woman's role of slave or wife, about her mother's "lies." She tells the hardest things on her list.

Suddenly she realizes that the only one really listening, the only one who needs to, is herself.

Only on her own, no longer dependent on her mother's strength or approval, can she both speak and listen, balance the silence and the talking-story, be the dragon containing both yin and yang.

She ends this book as she began, telling a story, this time not the story of a woman with no name, locked in a punishing silence, but the story of a woman in exile, captured by barbarians, a Chinese poet who sings until her children, who do not speak Chinese, sing along.

Kingston's story of a daughter's separation from her mother to find her own independent voice translates well for all of us with powerful mothers. Her story of first-generation trauma translates well for those whose parents are immigrants. Her whole book expresses her independence, telling the stories which from the first line her mother tells her not to tell, in order both to honor the dragon in her mother and to claim its power for herself.

Both Kingston and LeGuin are speaking to the danger of fixing the yin on women and the yang on men. Within one whole person both energies must be present and valued. The symbol gives equal value to each energy because yin and yang are continually changing into each other and cannot be separated. Whenever one kind of energy is attributed to one kind of person and its opposite to another, equality, flexibility and interaction are lost, not because of distinction or difference but because of hierarchical thinking and practice.

The concept of separate but equal, of complementary roles, cannot exist in a world where one role is more valued than another. LeGuin shows us a world where this distinction cannot be made in terms of gender because the person is in motion. Kingston shows us a whole culture in motion.

The Marriages Between Zones Three, Four and Five

In this fantasy novel, Doris Lessing shows us how the extremes of hierarchal thinking create stagnation and despair from top to bottom of what should be a whole organism.

Zones implies distinct areas as parts of a whole: the whole earth (frigid, temperate, torrid), a whole region (districts, neighborhoods, postal areas), a whole body. Although any of these wholes might fit Lessing's descriptions, the one which provides me the most insight is the analogy of the chakras, or energy centers in the human body.

As part of a Hindu healing system, chakra means wheel or vortex. Each center has its own axis of spinning energy. Each of the zones in the novel also has individual integrity, which creates the illusion that

CHAKRA POINTS

CROWN: Mysticism

THIRD EYE: Intuition

THROAT: Communication

HEART: Love

SOLAR PLEXUS: Will

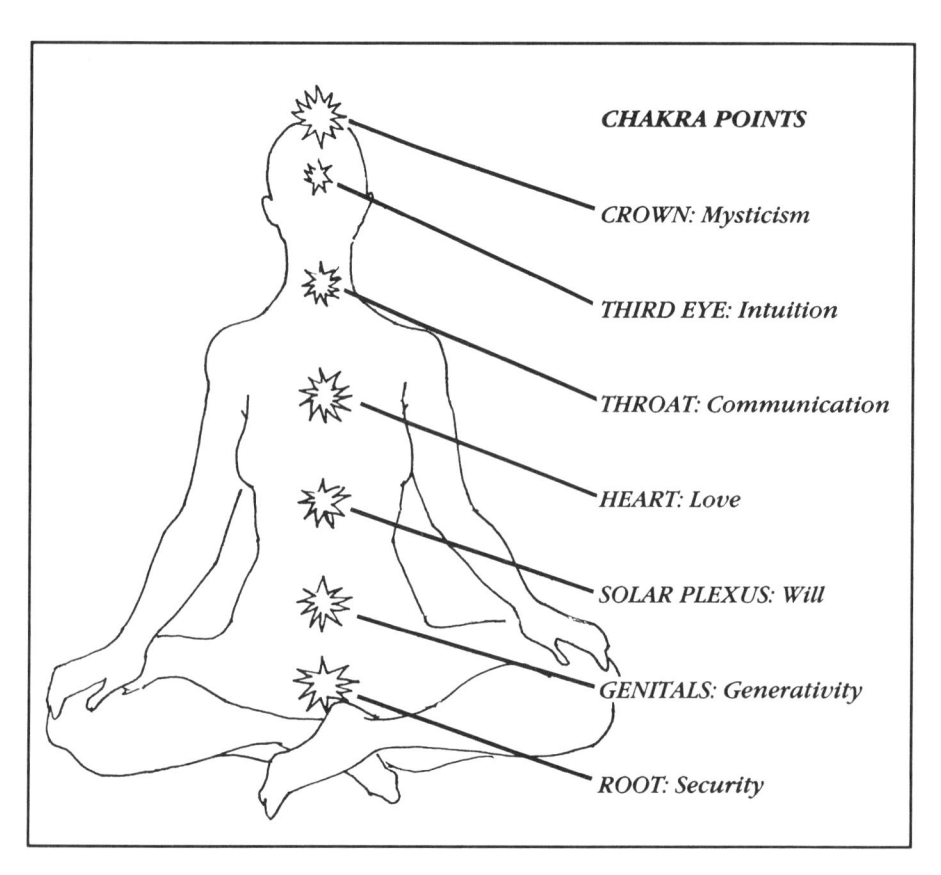

GENITALS: Generativity

ROOT: Security

each is independent of the others. It takes both a loss of vital energy and a message from outside to remind the inhabitants of each zone that they cannot exist apart from the other zones. Actual healing takes place only by "marriages" between the zones.

This fairly simple story is about Al-Ith, Queen of Zone Three, who is ordered by the Providers to marry Ben Ata, King of Zone Four. Just as their union is at its fullest, he is ordered to leave her and go down to Zone Five to marry its queen, Yahshi. Each marriage blurs the boundaries between the zones and brings healing to each.

The three zones in the novel correspond to the heart chakra (Zone Three), the solar plexis (Zone Four), and the sacral center (Zone Five). Al-Ith's Zone Three has the qualities of the heart chakra: peace, equality, ease, trust, balance, friendliness, sensitivity to feelings (as long as they aren't too negative), nurturance, ability to communicate with plants and animals. The heart chakra is considered "feminine," so its ruler is a woman. Ben-Ata's Zone Four has the qualities of the solar plexis: will-power, discipline, control, directness, conformity, possessiveness, duty, fairness, obedience to a higher power—many virtues considered "masculine." Vahshi's Zone Five is characteristic of the sacral or second chakra: raw energy, movement, sexuality and procreation, desire, aggression, emotion, self-indulgence. This zone is ruled by a wild woman.

Key to understanding the novel, as well as the chakra system, is that there must be a flow of energy between all the zones for each of them to be balanced. Like electrical circuits, the chakras form one energy system; if one is blocked or stagnant, all suffer. If there are solid walls between them, strictly enforced borders, the result will be the sterility we see in all three zones before healing takes place. In Zone Three, a seemingly perfect realm of beauty and harmony, the animals—cut off from the raw sexual energy of Zone Five and the willpower of Zone Four—"have lost the will to mate" (41).

In each zone we see how this dis-ease turns what is its characteristic strength into its weakness. The harmony in Zone Three becomes complacence, shallowness, lack of compassion. The discipline in Zone Four becomes militaristic authoritarianism with blind obedience or furtive rebellion the only options. The energy and movement in Zone Five become anarchy and destructive chaos.

Only after the healing takes place is the narrator able to observe the connections:

> After all, this story of Al-Ith has taught us all that what goes on in one Zone affects the others (142).

Interestingly, Lessing uses what seems at first a hierarchical tool, the chakra system, parallel to Indian castes, to diagnose this disease of hierarchy. Hierarchy thoroughly manifests itself in two societies where she herself has lived: the racist and imperialist Southern Rhodesia, where she spent most of her childhood (her father a military man), and the more ostensibly benevolent and peaceful England, where she has lived as an adult.

In the Hindu system one moves through castes by way of reincarnation, capable of achieving enlightenment at any level. In the world of Lessing's novel, movement must be allowed between the different zones. In her model a person can be surprised by liberation at any point.

The chakra system does contain the notion of higher and lower selves. The crown chakra is not only at the top of the head but also the source of our most spiritual energy. But what's healing about this system is that it reinforces the idea of each chakra or zone being part of a single unified organism, one whole person. Lessing signals such unity by her narrative structure which has no chapter breaks, no boundaries.

Lessing focuses on the microcosmic or personal aspect of the healing by showing us the transformation which occurs in Al-Ith as a result of the marriage between Zones Three and Four. First she must go through her distaste at having to "descend" to the "lower" realm where she is subjected to abuses generated by the energy imbalance there.

Gradually her grief and arrogance give way to an appreciation of her new husband and a connection with the submerged and subversive energy of the women of Zone Four. She begins to realize that she is on "the verge of a descent into possibilities of herself she had not believed open to her" (58).

Lessing's description of the sharing of energies between Al-Ith and Ben-Ata brilliantly chronicles the merge and synthesis which take place in relationships: the movement from mutual alienation to an exchange of energies to a shared exile from their former identities. Then ironically, when they have reached real equality, balance, true love, and they are "healed as if of some frightful and unnatural separation that had afflicted them" (189), the silence comes upon them. This is the silence of the drum no longer beating, a signal that they must go their separate ways.

This completion is, of course, the harsh wisdom of the yin/yang, of the changing seasons. As soon as fullness is reached, emptiness begins; as soon as union is achieved, separation starts. As poignant is the description of Al-Ith's subsequent transformation:

> She was not going to be accepted back into her old self or into her land.... It was as if she was being made distant from everything she had been, lighter, drier, more herself in a way she had never imagined" (189).

As we saw in the works by LeGuin and Kingston, as soon as an organism finds its own wholeness, it becomes dynamic in ways that bring it into conflict with the old world, the old matrix out of which it grew. The challenge and the grief of our lives is this mysterious fact of change. We can't return to our old worlds because those matrices themselves are changing. Belonging is always a temporary and relative experience, no matter how static our lives seem to be.

Amazingly Al-Ith's descent into Zone Four propells her forward, not home, into Zone Two, that blue and distant realm which fascinates her as soon as she begins to look back up from Zone Four. She must, as the revolutionary saying goes, take one step back in order to take two steps forward. She can't willfully leave the contentment and power of Zone Three, even though her personal growth is restricted there, without the energy and self-awareness she gains from Zone Four.

Zone Two corresponds to the throat chakra, which is associated with blue in the chakra system as well as in the novel. This is the area of personal self-actualization, inspiration, communication, the place where one finds her own voice. It's a realm one must venture into alone. This Queen of Hearts must first learn to affirm her masculine/shadow side. Then she must separate herself from others and go into the zone of self-actualization and communication. Socialization for many women seems to weaken both the solar plexis and the throat chakras. Healing into a deeper selfhood seems to require discovering our own will to personal power and our own voice.

By the end of the novel, there is healing for all:

There was continuous movement now [between the Zones]. There was a lightness, a freshness, and an enquiry and a remaking and an inspiration where there had been only stagnation (245).

By pulling these abstracted symbols of yin/yang and the chakra system down to earth and into the movement of time, LeGuin, Kingston and Lessing symbolically express larger wholes, not just one side, one culture, one zone. By showing us worlds and persons in motion, their narratives offer a critique of the uses made of these symbols by the patriarchy. Within its hierarchies the apparent perfect circle of the yin/yang symbol, the organic wholeness of the chakras cannot expand to include more and more diverse realities. Instead, they remain static and constricting.

Each writer affirms, without denying the pain involved, the necessity of change, the recognition that even the most expanded moments of wholeness are continually dissolving and reforming so that others more expressive of the new moment can be realized. A realization of each moment allows for what inevitably comes with change: emptiness, ebb and silence as well as fullness, flow, sound.

Each writer also describes transformation: the restoration of wholeness through a healing of splits, a unifying of fragments or a discovery through emergence of new forms. Each shows how transformation comes from the very realms which have been excluded or devalued: the exiled, the silenced, the step down or back. For instance, rather than polarizing the zones, as certain mind-sets of patriarchy would do, or even turning the hierarchy upside down, as certain anti-patriarchs have done, Lessing refuses the absolutist either/or. She shows us how the energy of the lower zone is essential for the health of the higher zone, in Al-Ith's journey backward in order to move forward.

In these works it is through the break in the circle, the unexpected gap, that the greatest change can come. *The Left Hand of Darkness* shows how growth has been stunted without the stimulus which must come from outside one sphere. *The Marriages* shows the stagnation, entropy, which comes from closed borders, set ways. Even *Woman Warrior*, which describes the pain of being caught in the gap between the diminishment of an old culture and the alienation of a new one, affirms the personal growth which emerges from that split.

Perhaps, also, as women we can accept change because of our intimate awareness of the process of birth: how new life can emerge from the crack in the egg, the split in the seed, the hole in our own whole. Knowing how we ourselves as women have not yet fully entered into the larger world or come out in the fullness of our potential, we can empathize with all that awaits in the Void to become part of a greater whole.

Midwives for the emergence of new stories through growth points within these ancient structural symbols, these writers have rescued the symbols of yin/yang and the chakra system from the absolute status with which the patriarchy fixed them to its own ends. Narratives like these, by women and others who have been excluded from the dominant culture, can revive and expand symbolic language for everybody. They transform what are often dead, because fixed, symbols into instruments of insight, even healing. Although rooted in ancient cultures, the symbols which shape these narratives give power to what are radical, contemporary and uniquely original visions.

CHAPTER SEVEN

Learning Intuition

ONE FULL experience of the intuitive process of integration, synthesis, creation and transformation occurred in a course I taught on intuition. On several levels, the students and I were able to experience and reflect on intuition together, so that we were transformed in the process. Some people say intuition cannot be taught, and perhaps this is so, but something valuable happened in this course that was unique and certainly intuitive.

Perhaps because of the traditional institutional context, a state university, this integration of emotion, intuition, personal experience, communal sharing and symbolic language seemed particularly potent. In varying degrees for different persons, syntheses occurred between inner and outer selves, between the intuitive and the rational, self and other, process and product, emotion and thought, subjective and objective, masculine and feminine, different disciplines, teaching and learning.

This course in intuition was offered through the women's studies program of Towson State University. Although the course was not called "women's intuition," the students were all women. I taught the class three times. The largest class, twenty-eight students, had the richest diversity, with ages from eighteen to sixty and differences in race, ethnicity and sexual preference. But in all three classes, whatever their size and composition, common themes emerged, themes of emotional integration, healing, creativity, trusting intuition, community, valuing the inner self, the authentic self.

The course was divided into four sections:
1. definitions of intuition, including my own, as well as discussions of what might be meant by the term "women's intuition";
2. an exploration of different people's experience of intuition from a variety of disciplines, writers, artists, musicians, psy-

chologists, scientists, inventors and philosophers;
3. cultivating our intuitive abilities; and
4. the creative process.

Three books were assigned: *Women's Ways of Knowing*, which provided a feminist framework for this as a women's studies course; Frances Vaughn's *Awakening Intuition*, which presents experiential exercises and descriptions of intuition from the perspective of transpersonal psychology; and a packet of materials on intuition which I put together from a variety of sources and perspectives. Time allowing, I would add an intuitive novel. I also showed a video on Georgia O'Keeffe's life and work and recommended a film on the Hopi, *Songs of the Fourth World*.

Students were asked to write personal responses to the readings in their journals. In addition to keeping journals, students produced three projects. The first was an experiential report on a tool of intuition. Students selected one or more tools from a list of options which I explained and, in some cases, demonstrated. They actually used the tool several times, reflecting upon that experience in a brief paper. Report topics ranged from symbol systems (tarot and astrology were favorites) and mandalas to guided imagery with music and various forms of meditation.

The second was a creative project, in any medium and with any theme. These projects usually grew out of a series of exercises we did in class or between class. They included paintings, interviews, tapes, stories, poems, plays, ways of healing. The third project was a final paper reflecting on some aspect of intuition—definition, application, creativity. In this paper they were to synthesize the intuitive process with more "rational" approaches, integrating, as a mode of translation, what was learned in the course with more traditional modes of thought.

These papers were shared at times with the rest of the class, either formally by reading or providing copies or informally by description or discussion. Exceptions were made for confidential material. One of the points I emphasized about intuition was how it perceives the whole through multiplicity, treasuring every unique experience, every different perspective. At the same time I pointed out the unusual opportunity within the class for sharing with a diverse group of people.

While these papers or projects were external manifestations of the process each person was going through, the internal process was expressed through journal exercises. They served as the basic circulatory, digestive and nervous systems of the course. These systems nourished a birth-giving process which often climaxed with the creative project.

On the first day, in the context of talking about intuition, I introduced students to intuitive language through an experiential exercise which took them briefly into the symbolic dimension. Between the first and second class, they responded in their journals to the questionnaire from *Women's Ways of Knowing*. These questions allowed each person to reflect on her own background, self-concept, gender definition, relationships, moral dilemmas, education and ways of knowing. I asked them to write an answer to one question from each section. This writing brought consciousness to the context of their whole lives, out of which specific issues began to take shape.

This context was then translated into intuitive language through a long exercise in the second class which took them through the intuitive process in relation to some particular theme from their own lives. The exercise encouraged them to tune in emotionally, find images to express their emotions, and then allow those images to play themselves out through the dynamism of a story. Invariably these stories were key to whatever issues the student chose to deal with in subsequent assignments. Often one central theme emerged in embryonic form: an illness, a conflict, a choice to be made, a problematic relationship, an unexamined trauma, a vision. This experience of the intuitive process in capsule form set the scene for subsequent transformations.

During the first half of the course students were not expected to share the results of their intuitive exercises, although some chose to do so. They needed only to record them in their journals. Some also reflected upon the experience in journals and in discussion. The emphasis at this point was on process rather than product, on deepening the individual's intuitive experience in whatever way felt comfortable for her. As we went along, it became clear that what was insightful for one (dreams, for instance) might be too elusive or unavailable for another. But by the end of the course, everyone had found at least one method or combination of methods which worked for her. This success encouraged trusting one's own experience and discouraged comparing self with others. They were well rid of such comparisons which were usually negative: "What's wrong with me? I can't remember my dreams!"

The variety of readings worked to the same purpose of encouraging choice. Each person usually found some material which spoke to her and some which did not. Valuing options myself, I tried to provide as many as possible for students. Choosing among the options became in itself a process of valuing one's own responses, while sharing responses in class exposed people to choices different from their own.

After the overview exercise, the exercises in the first four weeks were of three types: centering techniques (silence/sound, meditation, mandalas); demonstrations of tools of intuition (guided imagery, *I Ching*); and groundings within certain disciplines. For example when we discussed psychology, we also explored possible meanings of individual dreams and took personality inventory tests which told us how intuitive we supposedly were. When we discussed scientific intuition, we did an intuitive observation/identification exercise. When we discussed writers and artists, we did dream poems and drawings.

During this time of reflection and exploration, we also talked about women's socialization and women's intuition, particularly in relation to such issues as emotion, space/time awareness and permeable boundaries. Although I shared my questions and opinions, I did so in an exploratory way, reassuring everyone there was no party line and reaffirming the richness of a diversity of perspectives. Not only was this compatible with how I felt intuition works, it was true to my experience. At that point I had more questions than answers, and I found our open-ended discussion stimulating and enlightening. The distinction between teaching and learning blurred for me, freeing me to learn as much as I taught.

In the fifth and sixth weeks, the exercises sought to help students develop intuitive abilities. We started with a group exercise of sharing female ancestral voices (adapted from June Gould's work), reflecting on marriage, work, politics, sex, money and death. In addition to providing a challenge to empathy and imagination, this exercise led to a reflection on women's socialization through generations.

That discussion in turn led to a discussion of concepts of time and space, synchronicity, intuitive time and symbols of time from various cultures (spiral, tree of life, yin/yang, wheel of fortune, lemniscule, rainbow.)

A discussion of symbol systems and archetypes led to an exploration of goddess symbols. Using guided imagery with music, people imagined and conversed with a goddess figure of their own creation. Following the intuitive process of image giving rise to story, we then discussed various myths as preparation for a between-class assignment to write a modern version of an old story, myth, fairy tale, biblical tale. Focusing on women-centered myths, I told the stories of Inanna, Demeter and Persephone, Sole and Spider Woman. The stories students were to write didn't have to be finished products but journal notes for a story. In addition to providing some examples (Judy Grahn's "Descent to the Roses"), I played a tape from National Public Radio about Mother's Day, which provided through a collage of voices a multi-faceted reflection on motherhood, a major theme in the stories I told as well as in the stories my students were telling.

Class in the sixth week focused on the application of intuitive process to healing, problem-solving and ethical dilemmas. For healing we did an integration exercise. For problem-solving we did a synthesis and transformation exercise. We also discussed the transformation of imagery related to menstruation and menopause. During this period we explored transformation through narrative by listening to and discussing their modern versions of ancient tales. For social healing, students did an empathy exercise related to sexual orientation. For ethical decision-making, we did role-playing around the issue of abortion, trying to develop a contextual and intuitive approach to this polarized issue.

The last two weeks were almost entirely student-focused. Students shared their reports on tools and their creative projects. We discussed possible topics for the final reflective papers, which were due, along with a self-evaluation, on the last day. Although each student was encouraged to take her own route in these projects, the sharing and discussion, particularly discussion of final papers, pulled together many different insights.

Reports and Projects

For their reports on tools of intuition, students wrote about their experiences with dreams, mandalas, drawings, acupuncture, imagery for healing, runes, meditation, color healing, ritual, guided imagery with music. One person wrote about how she used creative visualization to help her get into her role for a play.

Some people combined tools. One woman wanted to explore a recurring dream image, so she used guided imagery with music and drawing to make the image more conscious, a process assisted also by her writing a report of the experience. Another woman combined a dream image with guided imagery and ritual, a ritual she shared with the class, to explore her grief over five miscarriages and the possibility of never giving birth to a daughter. Our actual participation in the ritual was moving for us and provided some closure for her.

Often the creative project grew organically, sometimes spontaneously out of the tools report. A person who tried dialoguing with dream images wrote a collection of dream poems. Another reported on a breakthrough with a cancer patient as a result of her reading. Reflecting in her journal on that experience helped her release the guilt she felt at not being there when her mother died. When she shared this report in class, she realized the guilt had blocked other unresolved feelings about her relationship with her mother. A week or so later she found herself at the computer writing letters to her mother which expressed some anger and regret she felt at the limitations of their relationship. These letters became her creative project without her planning it.

The creative projects were even more diverse and rooted in unique experience than the tools were. In some cases the intuitive process allowed for a greater freedom of expression. Two talented artists, who had returned to school after raising their families, remarked that this was the first time they'd been able to express in art what they really wanted to express in the way they wanted to express it. In art classes they were bound to draw what and how the teachers wanted. Their paintings were marvelous in conception and execution. One painting emerged from a guided imagery we did in class, an integration of the artist's masculine and feminine selves. The other was a synthesis of symbols of intuitive transformation, egg, spiral, butterfly.

In some cases people tried forms of expression they'd never tried before. One talented writer chose to illustrate a dream with simple but powerful drawings which tapped into the adolescent energy which the imagery was releasing. Another gifted actress challenged herself not to go with her known talent but to try something scary, drawing pictures of her multiple selves and then writing a poetic story which brought all twelve of her together. Others wrote poems and stories for the first time in their lives. For one person the process of trusting her intuition, despite blocks against her creativity, was as important as the final product, a painting of a dream image. Another person produced a collage of music and voices on a tape about dreams which revealed a creative talent she hadn't suspected.

The range of talent was wide. Some people had considerable skill and some took their first shaky steps into a new realm. Surprisingly, however, this gap seemed not so important in the long run. Perhaps because of the supportive atmosphere of the class and perhaps because individuals were usually pleased with their own creative process, they did not judge their products harshly.

In some cases, the process was so deeply tied to central issues of healing and growth that the product was the least of the results. One student used poetry to express her grief after being startled by her dead daughter's appearance during a guided imagery. Another tapped into her grief about a dying son in the process of sharing a tale and painting of a swan trying to rescue one of her babies. Another shared the creative process with her artist brother as a way of understanding his mental illness. Another wrote a story to help her describe her own experience of cancer. Others used modern myths to explore childhood traumas and expanded on exercises from class to integrate suppressed parts of themselves or to empathize more fully with mothers and grandmothers.

When I look back over each individual process from journal to report to creative project, I am struck by how certain issues run through the whole: a dying sister, a failing marriage, the care of aging family members, an abused daughter, an uncertain future, not enough time and too much pressure, conflict in a relationship, a frustrating job, a generation gap.

Sometimes issues were partially resolved. One woman who did mandalas for her tool report realized through them how unhappy she was. A guided imagery in class gave her a positive vision of an alternative life, but it wasn't until the last class, when she shared her poems which described the relationship she was planning to leave, that we realized she was the victim of considerable physical abuse. But even before writing the poems, she had taken major steps to change her life—counseling, a support group and plans to move.

More often issues were still being explored at the end. The woman who wrote about dancing on and breaking eggs volunteered to role-play someone who had an abortion, even though she confessed later that she was a devout Catholic vehemently opposed to abortion. Her creative project expanded the empathy exercise into a story told from the point of view of an articulate and appealing fetus suddenly cut off. On the rational level of the moral dilemma, her position was clear. On the emotional and symbolic levels, she seemed willing to explore the complexities of other sides.

Sometimes people solved their problems by reframing them through the creative process. One person's worked through a complex tangle of emotion tied into the burden of caring for aging in-laws. Another decided to stop pushing herself so hard. Another, out of love for her daughter, confronted the pattern of mother-daughter splits in her family by interviewing her own mother, from whom she had been estranged.

Some problems, like death, can't, of course, be solved. One of the most moving of student issues involved a dying sister on the west coast. This situation initially presented itself to the student by a story of herself as the rescuer. In another guided imagery, she had a vision of her sister's spirit after death. She also received a message from her goddess to go visit her sister soon. She returned from the subsequent trip west with her creative project, a taped interview, modeled after the ancestors' voices exercise we'd done in class. On the tape she'd asked her sister's opinions on marriage, work, education and death and recorded their discussion of these issues. The visit and the tape allowed her to help her sister in her dying process and gave her a wonderful way to remember her. She told me at the end of class that she thought this might have been the last time she was to see her sister alive. She was grateful to have recorded her voice and thoughts.

These projects confirmed my conviction that if you heal the language (by integrating emotion and intuition), the language can help heal you. Nevertheless, although healing, the class was not a series of therapy sessions. Allowing for the reality that good education is therapeutic and that good therapy involves re-education, being a therapist and being a teacher are two different roles, contributing to two different processes.

Students did not enter this class seeking therapy. Some did not want it and some did not need it. They did not choose me as a therapist, and they did not choose this class as a therapy group. They had a wide variety of issues, some asking for healing and some not. They also had a wide range of consciousnesses, maturity and self-awareness. Remarkably, although some became inspired by others to dig deeper into their own experience, no one complained of pressure to do so. Such pressure would not only have been unethical, it would have destroyed genuine intuitive process.

Nonetheless, what surprised us is how potent the intuitive process can be. Because intuition must be experienced to be understood, its impact for change is deeper than if it were just another subject to be studied. It releases and rides emotions and images which have been kept hobbled or bridled for years. It acknowledges and encourages the inner self, granting it equal status with outer roles and duties.

The potential integration of a part of self lost or buried can be tremendously healing, even if glimpsed only for a moment. Insights into a whole reality invite new syntheses, new visions, new creations. The expression of an insight in symbolic language intensifies its impact and gives it further validity. Sharing this expression with others expands its power even further. Some people do not realize the full implication of what they have discovered until they share it with others. Then the feeling flows; then the illumination arrives.

For some people, those with stories of abuse or neglect, the sharing can relieve a terrible burden of silence. For others, links with other people's expression can allow one to speak up. One African-American woman referred to the story of the aborted fetus [by another African-American woman]: "In the Black community there aren't that many happy endings." This was by way of transition into her story about a precognitive dream which actually came true, a modest version of the American dream for one Black family. Realistically she described the protagonist waking up not sure whether to be angry the dream wasn't true, no happy ending yet, or to trust the potential in the vision. Response in the class supported both reactions, but her own story chose a way out of despair.

Within this communal context, my own role became lighter. But even with that support, I never saw myself as a therapist. I didn't have the inclination or the patience to accompany each person down the long road to healing. I shied away from transference as surely as most teachers I knew did, even though I recognized that it happens all the time. Fortunately I had many years experience as an parent-alternative rather than a parent-substitute to draw on for this detachment. I saw myself as a guide and a resource person. I introduced people to tools and processes which they could use on their own for their own purposes. I helped them design maps to where they wanted to go.

I also kept myself informed about local resources for serious problems like incest, battering and mental or physical illness, so that I could refer people to support groups and counselors if they wanted them. On a one-to-one basis, I shared relevant personal experience. I trusted my own intuition to tell me when people needed encouragement to seek help and when they needed to be left alone. This sensitivity applied to their creative processes as well as their healing processes. Because so much genuine support came from within the group, I tried to facilitate group process and allow group interaction, acting as a buffer the few times someone intruded into another's privacy.

After years in consciousness-raising groups, support groups and women's studies classes, I have a profound trust in the fundamental process of self-expression and communal sharing, which is deepened and heightened by intuitive techniques. I myself cry easily, so tears do not disturb me, nor do they indicate anything pathological or in need of healing. They are simply a sign of emotion, an indication of healthy release. Although some students initially apologized for tears, no one was profoundly embarrassed or otherwise unable to handle her feelings. Often she would just hand her paper over to some sympathetic colleague (who might herself become tearful) to finish reading for her. I know myself what confirmation it can be to read something deeply moving and then look up and see tears in other people's eyes. This silent empathy was a potent bonding in a class where people did not know each other to begin with and might never see each other again. Tears were not the only adhesive. In some classes students cheered when someone expressed anger with which they identified. One of the strongest bonds was laughter.

Emotion was such a natural element in these classes that I can't imagine how real education can take place without it. But it is crucial for teachers to process their own emotions so they don't get caught in the trap of trying to fix a student's feelings as a way of avoiding their own. There is nothing we must do about a student's feeling except allow it to be (keeping at the same time one eye open for the potential of destructive action.) Rarely have I had to follow someone out of the classroom because she was sobbing, but even then what I did was pat her back and listen. It's what I would do with a friend.

Did the "serious business" of readings and assignments get lost in the trauma? Occasionally. But usually it was the few people avoiding issues who ended up making excuses about not having time to read the texts or write papers. The ones who, as Marge Piercy puts it, jumped in "head first without dallying in the shadows and [swam] off with sure strokes" (49), were grateful for all the buoys and rafts, maps and logs they could find by way of tools and texts. No matter how horrendous the issues people chose to deal with, there was something so exhilarating about the creative dimension, something so buoyant about symbolic language, that they momentarily forgot their problems in the joy of expressing them.

For me teaching these courses on intuition helped transform my experience of teaching. Twenty-five years ago, when I first started teaching, I knew that the best teaching came when the teacher was also learning. But I had not fully experienced, as a teacher within a formal educational setting, the joy of learning with, and not just at the same time. Whether because of the institutional context or the strictures of grades and roles, the contrast between learning in nontraditional settings and learning in traditional ones was painfully obvious.

Reentering the prosaic territory of the conventional classroom, I was prepared to teach a "new" language, the ancient symbolic tongue. I did not expect to discover, with my students, a new world. I did not expect to learn, in the process, that this new language is one most of us once knew and forgot, that this new world is for some of us our home planet. The blurring of lines between teacher and student was essential to this discovery, for one usually doesn't speak a language all by oneself, and very few explorers voyage alone.

Perhaps intuition can't be taught, but it certainly can be learned—even within a traditional school.

Final Papers

My belief that the intuitive process can be learned was reinforced by student reflections. The following are excerpts from final papers by students in one class (a different group from the one described through the journal entries in Chapter Four.) The students were asked to reflect on some aspect of the intuitive process and to translate their experience into a language that integrated both "rational" and intuitive modes. They were also asked to synthesize with their own insights four different sources from the assigned reading. Many students also integrated into that paper a personal evaluation of their experience. Each set of deer prints represents a different person.

Intuition. INner voice. INsight. Teacher withIN. How do we know intuitively? By looking within, by listening to the inner voice, guided by the inner teacher. Intuition is in me, therefore is me. Intuition is not external to me. It is not other. Yet paradoxically it is through intuition that I am everyone and everyone is me. Above all, intuition is the way into the true self.

The true self has many dimensions... How can we categorize the primal experience of Ruth Winji in "Harvest" as only physical intuition when what she takes in through her body is instantaneously translated to emotion and thought and even at times spiritual transcendence? Or Alice Walker's protagonist in "Everyday Use" who knows she has seen the truth and experienced the divine when she feels as if something has hit her on top of her head and run all the way down the soles of her feet and who always expresses such moments of spiritual physicality in wild emotional outbursts? What do we make of a Barbara McClintock whose "feeling for the organism" is simultaneously a deep emotional attachment, a physical identification, spiritual reference and mental understanding? All these women experience life holistically; all are holistic. In the final analysis their intuition cannot be analyzed, cannot be reduced to parts of a whole. It can only be viewed from all points on the circle and all at once... I feel confident that working on and developing [all] forms of intuition and those parts of myself that I previously have neglected and undervalued are essential for finding my center, for living a balanced and harmonious life, and for my continued emotional and intellectual growth.

Can seven Saturday mornings change a life? Yes. Although it sounds clichéd, that's what has happened to me while taking this course. Since I was a child I've always wanted to be a writer, to create, to leave something of myself on this earth in artistic form. But in one sense I was cursed to be an academic "star" and years of traditional Western education buried my creative, intuitive side under mounds of analytic papers and positive teacher feedback for verbal logic. This course brought me home to myself. With a suddenness and ease that still surprises me, I have reawakened my creative powers. They are a source of strength too. Or better yet, empowerment. As I began to write again creatively that focus and direction rubbed off in other areas of my life... The other wonderful experience for me has been the almost support group nature of the class. The collective strength of the women this semester has been awe-inspiring. I have truly felt blessed here.

This course has touched my life in ways that I had not anticipated. I expected to learn about intuition but I had not planned on being changed by what I learned. I thought that this course would be like so many others; I expected to sit through lectures, read my assignments, take the exams and get a grade. I thought I'd make casual acquaintances; I thought I'd like the teacher or not. But this course has affected me like few experiences in my life. This course has changed me in ways that will change the lives of people around me. I have changed because I have experienced on an intuitive level and I have learned to trust my intuition. I am so aware of intuition and of women who experience and feel intuitively, that identification with the women in the class and with the women in our readings seems very natural.

I had been raised and trained to take care of others and not to think of myself. But I realized that unless I was a whole person, I could not possibly hope to care for others; I learned that only I could take care of me. This course has taught me new ways of taking care of me, of nourishing me, of getting me in touch with me and trusting me.

This course has helped put me in touch with myself on a level I had not imagined. I feel more well rounded, I feel more in tune with others and better able to help them. When I look at my patients now, I seem to see them more clearly. I know that this clearer vision comes because I have met myself and I like who I am. This class experience represents one of the most meaningful learning experiences of my life.

I feel that when I began the course my soul was like a small sponge that was nearly dry. The course has filled the sponge with the moisture of intuitive learning and has allowed it to expand to the point of overflowing.

When I enrolled for this class I was not sure exactly how to define intuition, but I was very interested in trying to find ways to combine intuitive and rational thought. One of the most important things I have come to appreciate is that the opposition we normally construct between the logical and intuitive methods is artificial. As Susanne Langer points out, intuition is not a method at all but an event, the beginning and end of logic. I began to put this idea in practice in a theory course I am taking this semester. The assignments consisted of examining and critiquing various theoretical arguments. At first I tried a purely logical approach, but I was having real difficulty trying to make meaningful judgments about the theories. I have very little confidence in my ability to think through these arguments logically. Finally, somewhere near the middle of the semester, I realized I had been going about it all wrong; what I needed to do was first allow myself to respond to the theoretical arguments on a purely intuitive level. If I felt intuitively there was something right or wrong with a particular position, I would then think about it rationally and try to figure out why I felt the way I did. If I could not come up with any rational reasons for my feeling, I would persist. Sometimes I would have to think for days about a single issue, and often the insight would occur to me spontaneously, while I was thinking about something else. This experience has helped me not only to learn how to combine intuitive and rational approaches, but more important, to learn to trust my intuition.

I was also interested in exploring the possibilities of a more intuitive approach to anthropological field work. In reading Evelyn Fox Keller's essay on Barbara McClintock, I was impressed with McClintock's capacity to develop such a heightened sympathetic understanding of her plants that she becomes one with them. Like other social sciences, anthropology has neither the method for acquiring the kind of understanding McClintock has gained, nor does it have the vocabulary for conveying it. I have done a lot of thinking this semester about the limitations of science as a way of knowing, and I have come to the conclusion that of all the social sciences, anthropology might offer the greatest opportunities to develop intuitive or connected knowing because of its emphasis on capturing the "native" view. I believe the kind of connectedness that McClintock brings to her work is what makes it an absorbing and exciting career rather than a job, and I would like to bring the same kind of perspective to anthropology.

Aside from my professional concerns, I wanted to find out more about my own self. One of the best ways to discover oneself is through the sharing of experience with others. In our classroom exercises and discussions, as well as the readings, I was continually reminded that women of diverse ages and backgrounds share such a large store of common experience. Alice Walker's *In Search of Our Mothers' Gardens*, for example, might have been about any of our mothers and grandmothers. Although it is doubtful that any of them have ever had to deal with the kind of oppression and stifling of creativity that southern black women have endured, each of them (and each of us) has had to struggle to create their own personal conception of beauty and to "innovate their inner psychological structures in order to survive... within the dominant culture" (Miller).

As Vaughn points out, working on self-knowledge and developing intuition are not alternatives to working in the world, nor are they substitutes for rational faculties. On the contrary, they lead to a recognition that one is capable of both intuitive and rational ways of knowing.

This course has been a very rewarding experience for me, particularly the chance to connect with so many women at a similar stage in life and with similar concerns and problems. I am always pleasantly surprised at how open and supportive women are when they are given the opportunity to share their experiences in this kind of environment.

I cannot begin to tell you how much this class has done for me. I remember on the first day telling B., "I'm no good at this. I won't allow my mind to concentrate or become part of the experience." Boy, was I fooled. It's almost like a rebirth. I have a calmer manner and it helped me get through the semester better than before. (Last semester I popped Tums all of the time.)

Intuition is inseparable from self-awareness. To be intuitive, you must tune in to your feelings. To fully experience life you must be willing to take chances; intuition helps you tune into feelings the rational world tells us to ignore. Intuitive experiences expand our consciousness. Intuition helps us to understand what is real. You cannot force intuition to happen; you must allow it to happen. To make a commitment to understanding intuition is to commit to finding truth. You must be willing to know who you are, to be willing to stop pretending to be who you are not. This can be difficult in the rational world where we are taught to pretend that everything is fine, when it is awful.

I selected this course because it fit my scheduling needs and filled a General University Requirement. I really had no idea what it was about. I ended up getting more than a GUR. I have started to recognize what it means to be a woman and a minority. I learned not to force the intuitive process, but to let it unfold slowly, the way a flower blooms. I was awed by the intuitive responses of my classmates and marveled at their brilliance. My own experiences never quite compared to theirs; and yet I enjoyed sharing my stories. I discovered that despite my analytical nature, I am intuitive. I am beginning to realize that I must treat myself with kindness, to think more about the qualities I possess, and spend less time thinking about the ones I do not. I truly feel that to continue the process of developing my intuitive self, I will learn to live and not merely survive.

By my being aware of intuitive abilities and processes, my life can be more fulfilling for me personally. I feel I now have some tools to help me say "It's okay," or to deal with some moving experiences. Intuition has helped me to put things into perspective and to live my life my way and not as others want me to live. I feel by doing this, I am a better daughter, mother, nurse, and person.

Perhaps the greatest message that I've received in this class is that my intuition is always with me, and only I can choose to follow it or not. I believe that I've been aware of my "inner knowing" for a long time, but somehow it had taken on the quality of more a nagging voice than a spirit guide.

Through my meditation exercises, through my journal writings and especially through the creation of my dream tape I discovered the special gift of my intuition not as a burden to be avoided but as an access to experiencing worlds within that I didn't know existed. And this experience can relate to the artistic world that I encountered as well as to the "real" world that I create every day. And so, if I can carry even a fraction of the joy and passion I encountered during the discovery of my creativity into daily living, I probably couldn't ask for much more from my entire education! My creativity has never been recognized or encouraged and I feel truly blessed to have discovered it.

Not only have the guided imagery techniques sharpened my intuitive tools, but the creative projects also aided in this process. My first project with mandalas enabled me to draw the emotions I felt at that particular time. My drawings were powerful—yet melancholic. After I studied them, I "knew" that the time had come to take action in my life. As a creative project I wrote an anthology of poems. The poems evoked my fears, bitterness and hopes. Although they were extremely painful to create, the mere act of creating channeled the intuitive process. A heavy burden lifted as I created these words with my pen. By my experiencing all phases of the creative process, a feeling of knowing and a sense of oneness with myself grew. Lastly, the most significant path I took to shape my intuitive abilities was the actual interaction with my classmates. Each women possessed her own turmoil, her way to deal with those problems, and her own intuitive experiences. Each possessed great power and love, and I found everyone in the class to be fascinating. I felt a sense of "connectedness" with each woman.

Individual interaction with regard to the healing process was particularly moving for me. One woman had everyone hold hands and pray for her miscarried babies, while another spoke of her healing techniques in her battle with cancer. The class discussions on abortion and the roles each woman played provided the stage for empathy. To be open minded is to see from all perspectives and is an intuitive tool I have sharpened. These women have moved me in such a manner that I am sure I will long remember them and the effect they had upon my personal growth.

Awakening intuition enables us to see the choices available and is thus a liberating experience. At the core of our being, we know what is true for us. From this perspective, the intricate web of relationships in which we are enmeshed may be perceived as a pattern. This pattern brings one into identification with the whole universe. In my journey down the road to intuition, I have become a part of this pattern, a pattern of strong "knowing" women.

INTUITIVE ACTION

Introduction

WHEN I speak of intuitive action, I mean action which springs from intuitive insight. Stereotypically, persons identified as intuitive are labeled dreamers and dismissed as unrealistic or impractical. But dreamers or visionaries can include people like Diotima, DiVinci, Sojourner Truth and Gandhi, whose philosophical insights, creative projects, theoretical constructs, political programs have helped form, reform and transform cultures. What we have more to fear in these times is action whose source is not, at least in part, intuitive. All kinds of disasters, from starvation in Africa to oil spills in Alaska, result from a tunnel vision fueled by economic or political self-interest, by a failure to look around the next bend or take in the larger picture.

The examples are many and include every area of human activity. It takes only a modicum of intuition to realize, for example, that if some people dump upstream and some drink downstream, eventually everyone will get sick. If we destroy our home, we shouldn't be surprised when we end up homeless. The vision underlying environmental action, an awareness of the earth's complex web of interacting, inseparable, dynamic relationships, has its source in intuition. The concept of ecosystems, as well as whole systems theory in the social sciences, is intuitively based.

On a more profound level, the reverence Native Americans feel for the animals who provided them with food, clothing and shelter is worship which is deeply intuitive. To ally with nature rather than to be at war with her is action which has its source in an intuitive realization that our human nature is no less and no more natural than the nature of the plants and animals with whom we share the earth. Our interdependence is a question of the survival of us all.

Intuitive action is equally necessary and positive today in the arena of political conflict, as Forster suggested in *A Passage to India*: "only connect." An ability to connect, perhaps empathize, while clearly helpful in interpersonal relations, can threaten to undermine conventional, adversarial political associations. Witness the combat between electoral candidates in our own country, even within the same party, where character assassination is the name of the game. Witness ethnic cleansing. Yet one of the most effective political strategies of the twentieth century, Gandhi's philosophy of "satagraya," is profoundly rooted in an intuitive realization that shaming one's enemy is an invitation to endless conflict. Through his actions Gandhi showed how it is possible to maintain one's own position, one's own integrity, without forcing the other to "lose face," to sacrifice his or her own identity or integrity. Gandhi warns of the dangers of following a philosophy which is not intuitive, the win or lose approach with its potential for humiliating the oppressor or seeking revenge.

This philosophy in no way undermines the necessity of the powerless to assert their power, to fight back when necessary. The people of India fought back. For women in this country, by and for whom compromise and negotiation have been considered virtues, self-assertion is crucial. True, a complex balancing of powers is essential to maintaining families and communities, but what kind of communities of wholeness are we nurturing if we leave no room for our own authentic selves?

It is particularly difficult, and particularly essential, that our actions have an intuitive source when we deal with issues of war and peace. We must recognize others as multi-faceted wholes and not just projections of our shadows. We must recognize our own potential for greed, violence and cruelty. In the face of another's, as well as our own, hostility, respecting differences becomes almost impossible. The long view of intuition, however, shows how tenuous the boundary between enemy and friend can be. Who is "us" and who is "them" keeps shifting. Grounded in a vision of wholeness, we are more likely to honor the ambiguity and complexity of international relationships.

One of the benefits of intuition as a source of action is that it helps us see the action itself as one long moment. Each action has potential consequences for our children and our grandchildren and so on, down to the seventh generation of the Great Law of the Iroquois Confederacy. Ego, greed, the short-term solution, instant gratification—the sources of so much action now—can be dead ends when viewed intuitively. Not just because of the fickleness of fame and the fragility of fortune but also because isolated events tend to ignore larger cycles of contraction and expansion, emptiness and fullness has recorded for us. All too often, they deny connections in the web of events which link one person's gratification with another's possible deprivation, a moment of consumption with a moment of reckoning.

This is not to equate intuitive action with morality. A vision of the whole registers the contradictions, ironies and paradoxes of human behavior, as well as the obvious consequences. Folk wisdom is full of reminders that "the road to hell is paved with good intentions" and "the best laid schemes o' mice an' men gang aft a-gley." We know that one kind deed is not likely to erase generations of abuse, and we hope that one fit of temper will not erase a pattern of caring. We have seen instances where one bad act, one mistake, one failure can clear the way to redemption, discovery, compassion or wisdom. Intuition realizes that the same deed may simultaneously pluck a chord of harmony in one heart and strike a note of discord in another. Intuition realizes that when we stir a strand in the larger web we can shake ourselves up as well as move others. Intuition shows that events reach backwards and sideways as well as forward.

This larger vision can, at times, leave us in despair or unable to act. True, we can never see the whole of our movements or evaluate fully their complex reverberations, some of which may be quite the opposite of what we intended. But intuition allows us to see even moments of non-action as necessary parts of the larger whole, times to rest, receive, reflect. Within its awareness of the deeper rhythms of revolution and regression, progress and conservation, generosity and survival, intuition shows us when and how to act in tune with the larger universe of activity. It keeps us humble, in touch with our place in that universe.

This section of *The Rest of the Deer* explores intuitive action in three contexts. The first context is the action of building a house. This description shows how intuition translates into action as it integrates with other faculties, specifically emotion, thinking and sensation.

The second context is the action of building community. To show this process, I trace the theme of self and community in novels by Alice Walker, Virginia Woolf and Judy Grahn. For those of us engaged in the ongoing action of building and sustaining community, in our homes, on our jobs, in our neighborhoods, descriptions of community by these writers can infuse our action with wider and deeper kinds of understanding. Their intuitive recognition of diversity within whole communities, their refusal to fuse the many into the one, offer clues to how we can alchemically transform old melting pots into multicultural cauldrons of gold.

The third context is the application of intuition to specific social issues like abortion, drug abuse, health, illiteracy and education. The applications are fairly tentative, seeds for those more deeply involved in these, or related, issues to plant in their own soils. While each issues call for specialization, lack of expertise need not discourage the rest of us from becoming involved in solutions. As intuition shows us, as long as we are part of the whole affected by these problems, we are involved. With that in mind, I invite readers to consider how intuitive language and process, as described here or with your own creative variation, can apply to other crucial issues such as racism, physical and sexual abuse, homelessness and the economy.

What generations have done or not done will take generations to undo or do. But, as the Chinese proverb tells us, "All the flowers of all the tomorrows are in the seeds of today."

CHAPTER EIGHT

Building a House

> The dwelling, the interior space, is the classic symbol of the female body. Architecture is called "the mother of the arts" and may well have been invented by women (Lippard, 155).
>
> Space is an extension of the body, and biological as well as social experience influences a woman's preoccupations with the relationships among outside, entrance and inside (Torre, 69).
>
> The word ecology was coined by Ellen Swallow Richards from the Greek word for home, and much "ecological art" reflects a related need to "return" (Lippard, 197).
>
> Little girls in play modify the space in imagination rather than in actuality, a bush becomes a wall; whereas boys build walls, windows, roofs (Susan Saegert and Roger Hart, in Torre, 146).

IF I WERE a purely intuitive person, I might be content with visions of wholeness regardless of whether they were actualized. As it is, I find more joy than many in the contemplation of eggs and spirals and diversified community. People are chronically urging me out of some trance so I can pay attention to the dirt on my clothes. "She's gone again," some say affectionately, tugging me back toward practicality.

But no one is purely intuitive. Other parts of me crave the actual. I love the exhilaration of making something new, watching a vision take shape. Addicted to the creative process, I realize it involves more than just intuition. Intuition alone cannot write a novel, build a house or change an institution. It's more inclined to rush on to the next book, the next project before the first is finished.

Because we've already imagined something in a flash, we figure it won't take long to actualize it and then we get frustrated or impatient when in fact it takes much longer than we ever believed possible. Even purely artistic expressions of space, shapes which nobody lives in, designs which are suggestive rather than practical, require more than pure intuition to find embodiment, as any sculptor can tell you.

Once I learned to trust and value my intuitive process, I began to watch how it could be integrated into other processes, how it works with and modifies

Bernice drilling

other faculties like thinking, sensation and feeling. One place where this interaction was most instructive was in the building of an octagon house with friends.

The following is a partial description of that process, from an intuitive perspective, a view often missing in the realm of action. Intuition is frequently left to its trances despite its potential to give wholeness to other processes. We've all seen, perhaps lived in, houses which were built without intuition: practical but boring square boxes which take no clues from organic forms and which leave their occupants feeling caged. Even bee hives, proverbial bureaucratic condos, have hexagonally-shaped cells.

About ten years ago a group of us purchased fifty acres of land in the southeast corner of the Adirondacks. Collectively we could buy what none of us individually could afford. Most of the acreage is up a mountain side. The rest is woods with two streams running through it, one a trout stream (in the days, at least, before acid rain), the other coming from a beaver pond across a dirt road.

On the land was an old one-room shack, made of rough hewn beams, with a collapsed side room, or porch. Our realtor advised us to knock it down, but instead we cleaned it up. First we removed the old porch and carried out the debris left by hunters who had camped inside. We ripped out old wall boards, which were covered with newspaper, put in new insulation and electricity, finished the upstairs attic space and set up a kitchen downstairs (no running water). Eventually we built a new porch. In the process we learned the basics of carpentry, with the help of one of us who took a construction course. This all took place over several years. But for the most part building was peripheral to our living on the land.

We were hesitant about spoiling what felt like sacred space with permanent signs of our presence. So at first we camped, constructing only tent platforms or easily dismantled branch shelters, cooking our meals outside at the campfire, using the stream for an icebox and for water. We were in love with the land: the lively, singing, always changing stream; the hundred year old cabbage pines; the clumps of birch; glimpses of heron, duck, kingfisher and owl; encounters with beaver, deer, raccoon, and coydog. We merged with the land as quietly as we could, fasting and clearing ourselves with yoga, meditation and chanting; going on vision quests; hiking up the mountain; following stream beds or animal trails, discovering vistas, secret hemlock groves and rocks big enough for picnics. We communed with the night sounds as we sat around the fire, watched the moon rise over the beaver pond or lay in a field alert for shooting stars.

During this time we tuned into the roundness of the world around us, horizons opening up on all sides, the shapes of sun, moon and starlight, rounded mountains and ponds, birds' eggs and nests, spider webs. We began to play with shapes which reflected this sense of wholeness: weaving baskets, making stone medicine wheels, forming ritual circles, creating round gardens. Without conscious awareness our intuition took deeper root.

Eventually chilly nights and rainy days prompted us to build more substantial shelters. We made these to blend into the natural surroundings, each one reflecting the needs and personality of its owner and her relation to the land. One built a cozy pentacle overlooking the stream, open on one side with a fire pit inside. Another built a glass house, using old windows to enclose the roof and sides. It nestled next to the stream under two sheltering pines. Another built a beautiful wigwam, which served more as a ritual hut than a practical shelter. Over my fairly substantial square platform, I built a succession

Model of octagon

Octagon house

of roofs, the first a spiral of grape vines, the last (on top of the first), an eight-sided pointed roof (which gave me confidence that we could actually build an octagon roof). It was covered with translucent plastic. None of these shelters were useful after late October or, because of the bugs, before June. The pentacle has a permanent, snow-sturdy roof, but otherwise is open to the elements; the wigwam was never really covered; the glass house had to be dismantled; and my shelter lost its plastic cover every fall.

Despite their limited practicality, our shelters were influenced by the organic forms we experienced around us. They were also tuned to the emotional and intuitive needs of each person, as I imagine shells are aligned with their occupants. As each person found a shape which expressed her unique person, we discovered the joy of integrating intuition into our building process. For some, that aesthetic dimension was everything; for others, practical considerations were primary. But we all came to appreciate that creating a home has more to it than making sure we have walls and a roof over our heads, essential as those are. As the song says, "Give us bread, but give us roses." What worked for each individual eventually became part of our communal process when we decided to build a house together. Together we had to figure out what would express the wholeness we shared.

Every fall we packed up our cars and moved to warmer climes, migrating with the geese. But eventually several changes prompted us to envision settling more solidly into the land. Our community expanded, putting a strain on the resources in the shack. We would sit knee to knee for supper and doubled up in chairs when there were visitors. The land next to us, the field where we watched the stars, went up for sale, and the realtor threatened to cut it into smaller plots for development. Two of us settled into the shack for the winter.

We decided to use our expanded personal resources to buy the land next door and to build a communal house on it. A house would give us more space and would be better suited for winter living than the shack. Much as we preferred to build a house farther from the road and deeper in the woods, we realized that the cleared field was an ideal space for it. Harsh winters necessitate being close to the cleared road, more heating is possible from sunlight in an open field, and we didn't want to destroy trees to make a clearing.

Just as we had to agree on what kind of land to buy, we had to decide what kind of house to build. We wanted something as close to a circle as we could get (symbolic of wholeness and community), so we decided on an octagon which, because it turns a square into a circle, also symbolizes transformation. The octagon seemed fairly manageable. We'd heard of others who had built them, we'd actually seen some (they were popular at the turn of the century), and having worked with four sides, we were confident we could figure out eight. Eight also appealed because of the eight people relating to the land. Although only four of us actually built the house, the others became involved in various ways.

Next we decided how to situate the house within the field, what dimensions would fit the setting, provide enough space and still be buildable. We made sure there was water within digging distance for a well. We determined directions so that we could benefit from the southern exposure and shield ourselves from northern blasts. Then we started drawing plans and doing research. I took photos of other octagonal structures, concerned particularly with how the roofs were put together. I experimented with my own roof. Others read books and talked to local experts (most of whom thought we were crazy to build such an odd shaped house, with no right angles).

One creative moment in the planning occurred when two of us envisioned together a double roof, a system that would let light into the center of the structure, and allow for an inner walkway with windows to look out in all directions. I had concerned myself with design, drawing various possible combinations of floor plans and roof systems and supports. Bernice, who eventually became our chief engineer, figured out plans with actual dimensions, stress loads and detailed support systems. In other words, while I followed intuition, she followed a more analytic course, but when we shared our findings, syntheses like the double roof design emerged.

Once we had agreed on the basic ingredients, I put together a model out of popsicle and lollypop sticks gathered from the local schoolyard. This gave us a three dimensional possibility to modify or expand. Then we asked two engineers to check our blueprints and give suggestions. Their advice, while invaluable, was obviously not tuned to the intuitive and emotional truths underlying our designs. While we had to heed their structural warnings (although generally, they were less cautious than we were), we then had to adapt those realities to our sense of design and wholeness. At every stage of the process, we spent many an anxious hour worrying about and discussing the risks and rewards of following our own truths in these matters. At every stage, because of practical considerations, we had to modify our initial vision and find creative alternatives.

Because of the emotional bonding we'd done, the powerful intuitive sense of symbolic design we'd developed and our practical needs honed by years of primitive living on the land, we were not as swayed by expert opinions as we might have been had we arrived fresh on the land wanting to build a house. Because the experts were all men, with years of experience, drawing on a tradition of craft none of us had been introduced to and because we were all women, with only minimal carpentry skills and experience, it was a challenge not to be intimidated.

But time and again, if we stuck to our needs and our vision, the men would become intrigued, would respond to the challenge enough to want to help us achieve our goal and would bring a discipline and determination to the shared work that, in turn, strengthened our perseverance. We all ended up grumbling together about the absence of right angles, the uniqueness of each cut (not only were there no right angles, but no two angles were the same), and the just plain hard work of building anything. But we also ended up admiring together the unique beauty of what we were building.

This process was most evident in the construction of the fireplace. Because we wanted a natural stone fireplace, we had to search for a mason to help us build it; that kind of masonry is a skill that has become rare. In the meantime Ann, who was most passionate about having a fireplace, with a clear vision of what she wanted and a highly developed sensitivity to texture and color, designed a fireplace with a round opening, descending steps and a log wall. We loved the design but had no idea whether or not it would work. The creative mason we finally found was willing to give it a try.

We worked with him, at first doing drudge work while he laid the stones; we gathered stones, mixed and hauled buckets of mortar. It was the hardest physical work I have ever done. That, in itself, was transforming. Gradually he let us try a hand at laying the stones ourselves and our flagging motivation picked up. By the time we got to the inside visible part of the fireplace, where we planned to lay our favorites stones, gathered from around the country or found on our land, we were familiar enough with the job to have a sense of what could be done and what couldn't.

Before we started working with him, we laid stones out in a pattern which matched the original design, so we had a clear idea of what we wanted where. As the actual building proceeded, we realized we would have to be more flexible, creating options as we went along. But we also had to be firm with him when we wanted a certain stone set in a certain place or way. When we were clear, he was obliging, even when he feared it might not work (the egg-shaped keystone or the split rock we placed as wings on either side of the opening). As we became more and more delighted with how it was shaping up, he joined the creative process with us, following our pattern or introducing new elements. For air holes he designed two eyes above a rock centrally placed because it looked like a face.

This was not work any of us could do alone. And although it was slow, one could not hesitate or reconsider choices once the mortar was ready. As a result it was one of the most intense and collective creative processes I've ever experienced.

The building of the whole house, still not entirely finished, has been an expansion of that intense creativity. At every stage there has been acceptance of physical limitation without betraying our vision. We have discovered new possibilities with each new step. Respecting the wisdom of centuries of craftspeople while holding true to what we wanted while remaining open to challenges and possibilities we hadn't anticipated has been a transforming experience.

Working collectively has been an even greater challenge. It's one thing to respect differences when everyone is free to go her own way, more or less. It's quite another to honor them when we're working together on a process that is risky, difficult and totally unfamiliar to everyone. But it became clear over the long haul that we couldn't have done it without the gifts and talents of all.

My strength lay in visioning the original design and initiating the process. Before anyone else believed in it or was committed to doing it, I made the model and dug the first post holes. We all felt the need for more indoor space and a few modern amenities like running hot water and a toilet for visitors, but I was even more captivated by the vision of a communal house. I had to push others into believing that we could do it without making a mess of it, that we had a right to expand, that it would be okay even if it didn't turn out to be exactly what we'd always wanted. Then I had to slow myself to enjoy the process of playing in the holes, consulting experts, dickering over details of where the kitchen should go (for some it was central, for others peripheral), how to divide the space between private and public and so on. I have learned a lot from watching others work about my low tolerance for physical frustration. I've also come to appreciate my resilience under those circumstances. Most of all I've appreciated the excitement of sharing visions of new possibilities as they unfold, motivating us to further creativity.

Ann on the roof

Bernice's strength lay both in her willingness to consult experts of all kinds (not just engineers but also local craftsmen, hardware clerks and friends who'd built their own houses) and in her ability to understand what they were talking about. Her analytical skill combined with a gift for envisioning actual detail in her head led, with experience, to an engineering talent which guided us during the entire process through obstacle after obstacle. She had to endure our impatience with her worry, our lack of comprehension at times and my inattention to detail. Because she understood the problems more thoroughly than the rest of us, she felt burdened by the project, yet captivated by the challenge. Along with her creative openness and ability to envision new possibilities, she also brought a tremendous physical energy to the project and an eagerness to learn new skills, which carried us through some rough times.

Bernice and Ann on the roof

Ann's persistence pulled us to near completion. When my energy fails (often at a point of frustration), hers digs in for the long haul. What I regard as unendurable, where Bernice will turn to an expert for help, Ann sees as a challenge. Time and time again, she pushed us to finish something I was ready to give up on: the awful wire meshing we put beneath the floor, the heavy log we couldn't lift, the one stone that refused to budge. Her physical courage inspired the rest of us (or some of the rest of us) to climb over the roof or up a pole after her. This attitude carried over to encouraging us to follow our own vision, not to follow the expert opinion (which was often contradictory anyway). She always insisted we try something first. She was the one who designed the fireplace and she brought that sensitivity to detail and design to every aspect of the building. She had to put up with our impatience when we thought she was being too fussy or too persistent, or when we were figuring stuff out in our heads which she needed to see in actuality.

So's strength lay in her sensitivity to the relational dynamics between us, her insistence on process when we had lost sight of the bonds that had energized the project in the first place. She was repeatedly turning what had become drudgery back into play, into a form of relating, into the process of transformation that it really was. Although she is a skilled craftsperson herself, with an artist's sensitivity, attention to significant detail and desire to work on her own, she brought an empathy and humor to the process that made it lighter for all of us. Whenever our relationships became strained by the building, as they often did, she insisted we work on mending those bonds first or at least take a break and do something more nurturing. At the same time she offered many creative suggestions, often resolving some deadlock in the process. She had to put up with our goal-directedness, worry and interpersonal tension. Just her presence brought a wholeness to the process that could otherwise have been lacking.

In addition to us, many friends helped along the way, almost miraculously arriving with the tool, skill, information or energy we most needed. Although we ourselves worked on every stage of the process, numerous friends and family members provided vital assistance at each step. My dream of a communal structure, open, flexible and able to breathe, expanding and contracting according to need, has been fulfilled. Were there no house to show for all the work, we would still be blessed by the generosity of friends and by the fun of working with such a wonderful variety of people.

What I have learned from this experience is that we can do much more than we think we can, that failure is almost impossible if we are flexible and persistent enough, and that, even at full capacity, I couldn't do it alone.

And what about the almost finished product? How does it express our values, both the original vision and the truths discovered in its making? Well, first, it shows our commitment to synthesis and to process. We had to synthesize our ideas and ideals with each other's and with the surrounding nature and weather. Each element—the roundness, the encircling porch become petals, the capacity to see the night sky—had to be integrated into the overall design, each person had a say in that integration, and the larger context of nature was a constant consideration.

Not only did we consider the nature outside us, the nearby trees, stream, road, mountain view, we responded to it by clearing the old orchard to allow apple trees to grow, by planting a large circular, flower-shaped, eight-petal garden (actually we did this before even starting to build the house), by planting various evergreen and flowering trees around the site.

We also brought nature indoors, allowing for light from different sides and integrating natural elements, the four huge maples holding up the center of the house, the stones in the fireplace, the openings made to allow in starlight and moonlight as well as sunlight. One day, before we put the windows in, a bird flew through one opening and out a higher one, without batting a wing. In our design we have been guided by the Native American perception of "beauty behind us, beauty before us, beauty above us, beauty below us, beauty all around us," a truth we'd discovered from living in the woods with little or no shelter.

We tried to avoid the rigid division between inside and outside that characterizes so many houses. We tried to create a protective but permeable boundary between in and out, with as much access between them as possible: four doors, an abundance of windows, access to a view of four directions, a porch system that mediates between floor and ground.

Our commitment to process was evident in our willingness to wait for consensus before taking each step, no matter how much disagreement there was. We also realized one valuable lesson: if failure is impossible, so is perfection. We had to let go of the ideal if we wanted the reality. We were also committed to enjoying each stage of the process, rather than focusing just on getting the job done, although when December arrived, snow was falling and we were still constructing the roof, we did push that principle aside for a moment.

Respect for each stage of the process gave us experiences we might not have otherwise appreciated. For instance, while digging the post holes and fireplace pit, communing with various snakes and toads whose habitat we were disturbing, we decided to dig a hidden kiva hole in the center of the circle around a central support post. Although this could also serve in the future as a root cellar, it was primarily sacred space. We held a night ritual there on a night blessed by meteor showers and planted a crystal. That spot is now covered up by mesh and plywood and may never be revealed, but knowing it's there gives us a deeper sense of roots in this place. At another stage, literally, when the floor and fireplace were complete, but no walls or roof, we staged a night of homespun drama with masks and costumes representing various animals and images particularly dear to us, followed by a dance. And at the final stage of building, we allowed ourselves a fuller expansion of our need for comfort, especially in the winter months, by installing hot water, a compost toilet, a gas stove and a large refrigerator.

The shape of the house reflects our values in that it is, like a whole person, multifaceted and multileveled (from kiva hole to floor to lofts to catwalk, like an ascending spiral, like the chakras.) The center is empty, a receptive space consistent with our feminist and spiritual vision, full of light, flexible (it can be used for yoga, dancing or performances). Here we can create and express our unity.

But each side is unique, with no uniformity. The one facing south, for instance, is almost all windows, with an arch curving above them. In the northeast side there are a round window, a diamond shaped window and a box window. The wall of each private room was designed and built by the person who will inhabit it. In this way we express our commitment to individuality within wholeness. It is interesting to see how features of our separate shelters have been incorporated into this shared shelter.

Allowing both separateness and connection is evident in the division of private and public space. Although we were limited by space and money in expressing this fully, we were able to build in three private rooms (out of eight sections) and a meditation room (half a section). There are several spots for individual privacy, as well as several areas for small group conversation: the fireplace room, the open central area, and the front kitchen/sunroom. Privacy is also protected by the door plans. The front door, closest to the road and driveway, opens onto the kitchen, a place of hospitality. The back door leads from the fireplace room to the garden. Two of the private rooms have separate exits/entrances.

Until we actually live there, we cannot know how well this system works. Since most of us have lived communally, we know the importance of free coming and going, as well as privacy. At the same time we did not want to fragment our house into little private spaces like separate apartments. So we have a natural flow through shared space from front to back, with private space on the sides like wings.

The building of our house expresses our creativity, our faith, our frugality, our commitment to be involved in all stages of the process and our risk-taking. Within the limits of structural necessities, we expressed our visual and aesthetic ideas: the double roof with views of the four directions; the eight sides with our varied shaped windows (round, diamond, oval, arched); the archetypal fireplace. We built with faith in ourselves, each other and our shared vision, faith that what we made together would stand and fit together.

We also built with minimum expense, using salvaged or used materials whenever possible, accepting kitchen cabinets, sinks, windows from friends who were remodeling, lugging a cast iron bathtub from the dump, searching for bargains—and doing it ourselves. Although we did have valuable help, some of which we paid for (the well digging, the drainage ditch, fireplace mason, the electricity and plumbing, the last desperate stage of roof building), we worked as hard as anybody else at almost every stage of the process. We didn't hire anyone to do anything we weren't willing to do along with them, if we could.

Finally we proved our willingness to take risks. We risked sticking to our own design, following no one else's plan. We risked putting our relationships on the line. We risked making fools of ourselves. We risked making a mess or being failures. We even risked, at times, our lives, or so it seemed at crucial moments when I was clinging to the scaffolding or creeping out on the roof.

Fear

Climbing to the unnailed
scaffolding twenty feet up,
I cling to the beam,
my knees sputtering
like water from a frozen faucet.
Clutching the hammer,
reaching into my cramped pocket
for the nails,
I spot a spider
swaying from a rafter.
Spiders, I tell myself,
are not afraid of heights.
How she got there,
how she'll get down
are far from her focus
as she rappels
off the edge of the wood.
Rope she spins
from within herself.
Rope tightens around me
like a noose.
Or I trip over it
and in my mind
fall the full
and fatal flight.
But when I follow
the spider's lead

> and tie a cord
> around my waist,
> firm, not tight,
> lines pulse from my center
> to form this web.

Despite the risks, throughout the process we honored and trusted our intuition as it helped shape the design, as it allowed us to value the diverse gifts we each had to offer and as it expanded to consider the whole context of nature and community within which the house lives. Intuition alone did not, could not, build this house, but without intuition it would not be the special place it is.

Having had this experience, as an intuitive person I know I will no longer be satisfied with mere visions of wholeness. I want to continue this process of construction in other areas of my life. Admittedly intuition prefers to start with emptiness rather than having to dismantle already established structures, like educational and social institutions. But intuition also loves change: each new actuality opens up new possibilities, each new dimension allows for new visions of wholeness. Having constructed the double roof, we realized the circle inherent in the catwalk.

Just as putting in windows allowed us to envision new connections between inside and outside, so too contemporary movements which open up questions about race, gender and class allow new connections between social institutions and wider worlds. Intuition, perhaps, is less concerned with demolishing old ways than are the faculties of thinking or emotion, which cry out for justice or analyze needs for change. Intuition, perhaps, can help us find ways to transfigure without destruction. Not as skilled as thought or feeling at documenting abuses or securing civil rights, intuition nonetheless has an important role to play in creating the kind of community in which rights can move from obligation to respect.

I'm still fond of egg shapes. I enjoy imagining the impossible task of constructing an egg. Before we built the octagon, I wondered how to transform a square into a circle. In another vision of mine, an artist, like a basketmaker, ties together two huge ovals. The horizontal oval represents a communal dimension: people sitting in a flexible circle with equal access to the center. The vertical oval represents the passage of time, the cycle of life. The whole shape, like a planetary orbit, allows for the pull of forces other than just the one at the center.

Painstakingly the artist sews together patches of cloth which, like a parachute or tent, cover this frame of ovals. After she sews the last patch, wind fills the shape and blows a flap closed. She is inside what has suddenly become an egg-shaped balloon.

What actually takes shape goes beyond her initial intuitive vision, but that form wouldn't be actualized if she didn't take steps to express that vision. As she integrates the two dimensions of space and time and synthesizes multiple pieces of cloth, a transformation, through the unpredictable agency of wind, takes place in the shape itself. Because she is inside that shape, transformation takes place for her as well. She isn't just the one who creates it but also the one created by it. Emerging from the egg of her own creation, she will be a different person.

Standing inside the home we built, we already feel some transformation. We have integrated our adult masculine selves. We are no longer girls who build only imaginary houses. But we have not betrayed our feminine vision. Knowing we can do this carries over to other work, other long term projects. The faith and stamina to write this book, for instance, was inspired by our house-building.

We have still to discover what transformation might occur from living within this house we built. For one it means having, at last, a room of her own; for another, having roots of her own, a house that will not vanish forever in the rear view mirror; and for another it means having a family of her own.

These transformations are what happen when we integrate intuition into our overall process of creation, whether we are actualizing a dwelling, a work of art, a way to survive, an educational reform or a social revolution. The more all our powers, intuition, thinking, emotion and sensation, cooperate, the fuller we will engage with the rest of the world and the more effective our actions will be.

Entering into it, gaining insight from the inside as well as the outside, we ourselves can be turned inside out. Actualizing it with others we become, together, so much more than the sum of our parts.

CHAPTER NINE

Creating Communities

AS CONTEMPORARY Americans, many of us connect to multiple communities. Despite the freedom and flexibility this can provide, tensions between self and group within our intimate clusters are often fraught. And conflicts within the larger communities of family, neighborhood, school, workplace and city over issues of race, class, gender, ethnicity, sexual preference and ability continue to plague us all. This tension and conflict is particularly troublesome for those nurturing persons who feel an intense responsibility to harmonize relations and to care for others, sometimes even at the expense of their own well-being. Many of us are painfully aware of the extent to which hierarchical thinking has poisoned human connections, but we're so deeply involved in the struggle for healthy relationships we find it hard to take time to sit back and look at our communities as whole systems.

In their fiction, women writers have taken time not only to contemplate their communities but also to describe them. Using the symbolic language of intuition they can understand these communities as whole, actual, dynamic contexts. In this chapter I explore how three womanist/feminist writers, Alice Walker, Virginia Woolf and Judy Grahn, describe their communities. Each of them deals with issues of individuality, inclusion, diversity and change within specific contexts. Each of them intuitively structures her narrative around a vital symbol. These symbols, like onions, contain multiple dimensions within one entity, allowing for full intuitive exploration of a whole pattern.

The Color Purple

Implicit in Alice Walker's *The Color Purple* are two related structural symbols, the rainbow and the wheel of fortune. The rainbow symbolizes diversity with unity. The wheel of fortune represents the inexorable rotation of destiny. For Buddhists, this ancient image symbolizes *samsara*, suffering from the illusion that we are going somewhere when in fact this karmic wheel goes nowhere and never stops. For some goddess cultures, the wheel represents the turning of seasons and life cycles, along with the wisdom of learning how to participate with rhythms of movement and rest rather than striving against them. For medieval Christian societies the wheel of fortune represented the complex and shifting interaction of luck, fate and providence.

Walker connects these two symbols through color. Imagine a cross section of the rainbow. It becomes a color wheel. By infusing the wheel with color, Walker transforms it from an archetype for the twists of fate into a vehicle for social justice. By choosing to ride the wheel as a community, people once excluded from privileged social levels include themselves.

Both the rainbow and the wheel are symbols of potential wholeness, the rainbow because it include all colors of the spectrum and the wheel because it is a circle, itself symbolic of the whole. But in the real world, some colors are valued while others, like brown and purple, are scorned for what they represent: people of color, people who are gay. The wheel of fortune seems stuck in the mud of racism, classism, sexism and homophobia, crushing those on the bottom of the social hierarchy. *The Color Purple* affirms the devalued colors. It shows how people kept down by oppression can ride the wheel of fortune toward their own personal fulfillment and communal transformation.

As Susan Willis points out in her essay, "Black Women Writers," color is much more than a visual phenomenon for African-Americans. She quotes from Toni Morrison's *The Bluest Eye*: "It be rainbows all inside." Color is valued by these writers for its vitality. The rainbow also has wide appeal politically as a symbol of inclusiveness.

For Alice Walker, the color purple symbolizes everything that is devalued, ignored, stepped upon—like Celie herself—poor, Black, ugly, female, lesbian: "I think it pisses God off if you walk by the color purple in a field somewhere and don't notice it" (167). Highlighting both purple and brown in the spectrum of colors emphasizes how the rainbow is like a color wheel. Completing the circle connects the purple border of the spectrum with its far edge, red, by way of brown, which shares characteristics of both red and purple. Arranged in a circle, the colors are of equal value whereas a hierarchical color chart would judge some colors as better than others.

While the rainbow symbol provides the guiding light of this novel, the wheel is its structural principle. Drawing upon the literary tradition of comedy, Alice Walker sets her novel within the framework of the bottom half of the Wheel of Fortune circle. Comedy assumes that what's been down so long is bound to turn up.

That this novel is a comedy might surprise readers who were moved by Celie's suffering. But comedy is often grounded in tragic events. Critics who found the novel's twists, turns and happy ending implausible could have looked to Shakespeare's comedies as a model. Here are the conventions which make this novel so delightful and surprising: mistaken identities ("Pa is not our pa!"), sisters separated and reunited after thirty years, play with bisexuality and gender switching, people drowned in storms and resurrected, everyone who lives being somehow redeemed, including Mister, everyone celebrating together at the end. It's a tribute to Walker's skill that these conventions have not been recognized as such in her novel. But to appreciate the tone and texture of her achievement, it helps if we recognize how they contribute to the overall pattern.

As Susanne Langer describes it:

> Destiny in the guise of Fortune is the fabric of comedy... [It represents the protagonist's] triumph by wit, luck, personal power. Comedy is an image of human vitality holding its own in the world amid the surprises of unplanned coincidence (331).

In this comedy the protagonist and all those connected to her ride the wheel of fortune past the nadir point and on up. Celie starts at minus zero, a victim of rape and incest, an illegitimate mother who loses both of her children after the hardship of pregnancy and the pain of labor, a slave to her father and to her husband, abused and ridiculed. By the end of the book, she affirms her own survival, she is with the people she loves the most, she has her own successful business, she owns her own house, she is fulfilled and renewed.

Joseph Campbell has remarked that if one rides the Wheel of Fortune at its hub rather than on the rim, one feels more centered, less subject to the extremes of fate or fortune. But that insider position may not be available to those who live on the margins of society. The other day while watching the news on TV, I heard an older African-American woman whose best friend had just died in a house fire say, "There's nothing out there in the world for us, but we enjoyed life."

Even though Celie does find something out there in the world for her, her deepest fulfillment, her triumph over fate, comes through

Tragedy

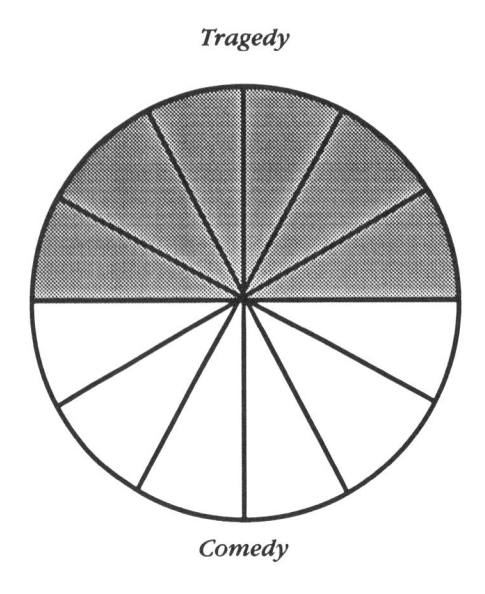

Comedy

her self-affirmation, her ability to love, her capacity for enjoying life. She is truly a survivor and, as Joseph Meeker explains in *The Comedy of Survival*, survival is the essence of comedy.

Even though the evils of racism, sexism, imperialism are realistically shown in the book, life goes on. The comic zest for life rises above the tragic consequences of being on the bottom rung, looked down on even by your own folk who are one step higher. When the wheel turns, the ladder tips. Even a villain like Mister can be saved because, as Langer puts it:

> The real antagonist is the World... The personal antagonist... is rarely a complete villain (349).

Mister Albert is mean, but he's not hopeless.

What saves Mister is that he is family, a member of the larger community which shares in Celie's "temporary triumph over the surrounding world" (349). The exhilaration of comedy, Langer points out, is that it gives us a vision of "a whole world moving into its own future."

Written in 1982 in the wake of the Civil Rights movement, this novel celebrates the expanded, though still limited, opportunities of its characters. As the song goes, "Been down so long it looks like up to me." From this perspective:

> the Wheel of Fortune signifies a high point, a wish coming true, the manifestation of something anticipated (Noble, 88).

Two key passages in the book indicate the kind of transformation Walker describes in this novel. It's not an African-American version of the Horatio Alger myth, the American Dream come true, but a transformation of consciousness. One is the passage in which Celie is fed up with God and Shug shares her vision of the divine. She redefines sinners as those who "do the best us can to please [God] with what us like" (165). And she pictures a God with kinky hair who is "inside you and inside everybody else. You come into the world with God" (166).

The second sign of transformed consciousness is when Celie finds out that the Olinka people worship the snake:

> They say who knows, maybe it is kinfolks, but for sure it's
> the smartest, cleanest, slickest thing they ever seen (233).

Realizing how in our Eurocentric culture the snake is a vessel for people's projections of evil, she concludes that the only solution is for every creature to be accepted as a relative.

When Celie and her community ride the Wheel to a better fortune, they bring along God and the Devil as well. This refusal to accept the polarization of good and evil, black and white, divine and human is key to the comic vision of the novel. It is the fruit of Walker's intuitive insight into the whole context she describes.

Intuition shows us, furthermore, how comedy completes a circle of which tragedy is only the top half. Tragedy, as Joseph Meeker points out, is often equated with a privileged class and a limited cultural perspective. It tells the story of a superior man brought down by flaw, chance or misfortune. Intuitively we know that below and in the background are many more persons judged inferior whose stories about error and loss can be just as meaningful. By pulling such experience into the foreground and by witnessing the ascent of some of these oppressed people, intuition gives us insight into a more complete experience. The bottom of the wheel turns upward as the top rolls down. Thus, intuition erases the line between tragedy and comedy, dissolving the isolated arch of the tragic fall into a grounded whole which allows for the balancing and healing perspective of comedy.

Alice Walker intuitively transforms these symbols of rainbow and wheel to serve the vision of more inclusive social structures. In the process her story offers a few remedies for healing some of the wounds in our communities.

The Waves

Although their characters are from different backgrounds, both Alice Walker and Virginia Woolf keep community central to their focus.

Walker shows how the "least among us" (although the best in terms of love, loyalty and courage) must be given equality before true community can exist. Woolf uses a communal protagonist to show how interwoven lives can be and to explore the issues of difference and change within a shared context.

Halfway through its incubation process, Woolf turned *The Moths* into *The Waves*. This change in image provided the structure as well as the imagery for her novel. It also signalled a major shift in her consciousness. Symbolic of the one and the many, the flame and the moths (which are drawn to the flame and disappear by means of it) represent a consciousness in which unity and multiplicity are two separate realities. With the image of waves both unity and multiplicity emerge from the same element. This symbol expresses how individual moments and unique personalities rise up out of the ocean of communal life and fall back into it in a constant rhythm of separation and union.

Waves are the individuating aspect of the ocean. In the novel they represent the separate personalities of the six protagonists as well as the unique moments they sometimes share. The ocean represents what they have in common, as well as the commonality of daily routine. Waves do not exist apart from the ocean, just as each person does not exist totally apart from the others. Each special moment falls back into the ordinary cycle of life, the daily rising and falling of tides.

The repetitive motion of waves and the expanse of ocean provide us with a sense of order, something reliable, enduring, unifying, the rhythm of continuity, sometimes of dullness. The fluidity of the waves, the way they rise and crash in unpredictable shapes and forces, speaks about changes in life, suggests a different rhythm, one of variety and potential threat. Both rhythms can cause destruction; the waves crash against the shore or wear away rocks by their daily pulsing. Some of Woolf's characters equate doom with the unpredictable while others experience a kind of death in sameness. The tension of the book is tied to these polarities: stasis/growth; stability/transience; the habitual/the genuine; dullness/doom; solidity/fluidity; community/individuality.

Through the multiple perspectives and fluctuating moods of the characters, we measure shifting dimensions of the same reality. If you look out at the ocean instead of concentrating on its edges, you see sameness and apparent solidity rather than the variety of its waves. If you shift your attention to the waves, you can feel how violently they might toss you around, how tumultuously they change. One of the paradoxes Woolf explores in this novel is how destructive solidity can be. Order and oneness can annihilate self, either because one fits in too well or because one doesn't fit in at all. Chaos, on the other hand, if it doesn't entirely destroy, can generate authenticity.

It was Woolf's intention, expressed in her diary, to unify the novel "by rhythms chiefly" for "a saturated unchopped completeness" (163). These rhythms shape both structure and style of the novel and establish the patterns of progressive change which give the book its deepest meaning. There is a progression from dawn to darkness. There is also a progression from childhood to old age. Each moment, each day, each lifetime is represented by a wave in a cyclical rhythm which promises to repeat itself.

Within these general rhythms are special moments. Sometimes they are shared—childhood, reunions. Sometimes they are experienced separately by the characters. Each has both a common element (a stage of life, a shared memory) and a unique aspect. Even when they are together, no two characters have exactly the same experience.

This rhythm of waves creates the books's collective protagonist. Commenting on the initial critical responses to the novel Woolf writes, "Odd that they...should praise my characters when I meant to have none" (*AWD*, 175). What she means, I assume, is that she intended to submerge separate characters into the rhythms of their common life, much as waves rise out of and fall back into the ocean.

Just as rhythm connects characters, it also connects larger elements of meaning. The reader who expects continuity to come from plot will be disappointed. What connects one section to another is primarily a progressive rhythm. One way of looking at the overall pattern of the book as well as its progressive rhythm is to compare two of the restaurant scenes. These are times when all six characters are gathered together for a meal, before and after the death of their friend Percival. What we see here is not just the difference between their youthful ambitions and actual achievements, but how the unity between them has changed.

The unity in section four has its source in Percival, the hero who "imposes order," whose adventures in India can be vicariously experienced by the rest of them. In what Rhoda and Louis recognize as a blend of cannibalism and the eucharist which foreshadows his death, they ritually devour him with a kind of patriarchal hero worship.

Despite this unity, much tension exists between the six. Although moved by Percival to a mutual summing-up, a chorus which heightens their sense of oneness, each is still egotistically pecking at her/his own shell. Each is separated by envy, pride, hatred. Each is preoccupied with self. Even though they see the falseness of measuring "I am this, I am that," they can't help clarifying with judging and comparing minds the differences between them. And even though before Percival comes there is a completion in being together, they rely on monolithic Percival to give substance to their unity. But as Jinny realizes, they will never "make this moment out of one man again."

In the second restaurant scene there seems to be little unity. It's as if Percival's death shattered them. Meeting is still a shock. They still feel the competition, envy, need to impress or tear another down to preserve self-identity. But mellower, after they experience the initial clash, they become more accepting.

What unites them is the silence which falls between them, the recognition of annihilation, chaos, death. They have been forced by the loss of Percival to ask what happens after the wave breaks. Although their responses vary, they are all pitted against "time's fangs" and try together to capture the present moment. This bond of mutual vulnerability, based not on an ideal or a person, becomes their source of unity, echoing the unity they felt as children.

After this drop of time has filled and fallen, they shrink back into their separate selves. Now instead of Percival, the heroic ideal, whose vitality made their lives seem safe but drab, they define their lives against the image of "small shopkeepers," whose drab existence gives vitality to their own. They return to the consoling rhythms of their lives, the must, must, must which shields them from those moments of silence which reveal the chaos, the void.

In contrast to these two scenes where all six are together, there is the final scene in a restaurant where Bernard is alone. Instead of a mutual summing up, Bernard is trying to speak for them. He alone has the gift to discover in their story something that has roundness, weight, depth, the fruit of their lives, the globe of their union. He realizes "I am not one person; I am many people... Jinny, Susan, Neville, Rhoda, Louis... I am you" (377). Because he knows this, he can make a "moment out of one man," can become "the body of the complete human being" they individually failed to be (369).

Paradoxically, since he himself is not heroic, Bernard identifies with Percival at the end. But Percival, who rode through India "applying the standards of the West" (269), an imperialistic idol, died an ironic death, his horse tripping (possibly in a polo game) and toppling him because the saddle wasn't tightly cinched. Bernard, on the other hand, who wishes to "be harnessed to a cart, a vegetable cart that rattles over the cobbles" (304), dies an heroic death, "unvanquished and unyielding." An old man he rides the wave, the great beast of change which stamped Percival beneath it.

Not the born hero like Percival, a figure of authority and idealistic projections, Bernard is the actual person, subject to failure and weakness. He is flawed in many ways and his courage comes after a long process of dying to self, being knocked down by the waves and getting up again.

Symbolically each wave seems to stand for a unique moment, an authentic moment. Sometimes this authenticity signifies individuation of personality, sometimes unity among friends, sometimes the loss of self which leads to a mystical vision. At the end, the wave symbolizes Bernard's rising to meet death. Each wave is an intuitive moment, fully charged with meaning. In Woolf's own words: "What I want now to do is to saturate every atom...to give the moment whole" (*AWD*, 143).

While the image of waves forms the structure of the book, the rhythm of waves is key to the style of the novel. Woolf makes her voice into the common element, the unifying energy, the water from which both ocean and waves are formed: "The human voice has a disarming quality, (we are not single, we are one)" (221).

Voice, more than perspective, has the potential to become such a unifying field. Although one person cannot at the same time see exactly what another person sees, both can hear the same thing simultaneously. Voice unites while sight distinguishes. Voice is more personal than vision. It connects the subject listening with the subject speaking and can be therefore more compelling. One can more easily shut her eyes or look away than shut her ears. As a medium, voice can also permeate other levels of reality, the emotional, the unconscious, the mystic, nature, even silence.

Woolf is not interested in personal idiom as such. What interests her is expressing unconscious organic unity, the vital force which the characters all experience, while at the same time allowing for diversity of personality, feeling and perspective. Operating symbolically rather than realistically, this voice can present us with a more total response, not just what the character would know or tell us about herself, not just what others might tell us about her, not just what stream-of-consciousness or interior monologue might reveal. The speaker is able to show us the pre-verbal as well as the verbal. Her voice records what people do but don't think, think but don't say, say but don't mean, mean but don't feel, feel but don't do.

This may be why Woolf said she had no characters. JoAnne Frye's definition of character as "perception, subjective presence and openness to change, as process rather than product" (64), is consistent with Woolf's own feminist strategies for expressing consciousness while bypassing fixed and determinist identities for women.

Although she finds a balance in this voice between the implicit and the explicit, Woolf seems personally to prefer the pole of change, variety and multiplicity (meanings which can't be pinned down) to the pole of sameness and stability (order, logic, linguistic certainty): "What I love most, change ahead." Perhaps this is a measure of how much she identifies, as a lesbian, a feminist, an incest survivor and a mental patient, with the marginal rather than with the solidity of class privilege into which she was born.

Even though Bernard, the character who emerges as central to the author's own values, is male, the novel itself, with its emphasis on rhythms and permeable boundaries, expresses the woman's perception from which it was written. Discovering in the image of waves intuitive coherence between her experience and symbolic expression, Woolf was able to describe in this novel some of the most poignant issues regarding self and community: death, competition, change, conformity, levels of unity, aging and authenticity.

Mundane's World

Judy Grahn's novel has at least three things in common with *The Waves*. It too provides unity through voice (more in the style of Gertrude Stein). It has a communal protagonist. And it builds on a natural symbol, the spiral. Like the chambered nautilus or the unfolding seed pod, the spiral is both image and record of growth.

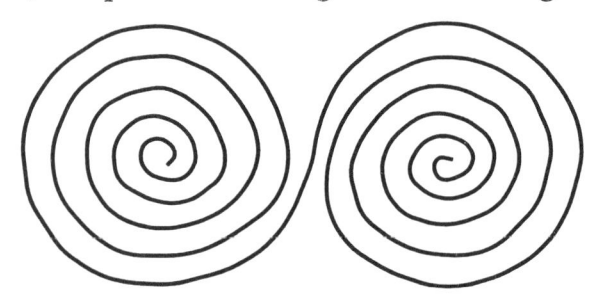

Mundane's World is about communal transformation, not magical, extraordinary changing of form, but the ordinary coming of ages of beetles, flies, owls, mice and girls. The spiral shapes and guides this transformation.

Rainbow, ocean and spiral have symbolic roots in ancient cultures and in the collective unconscious. Because most of us have actually experienced rainbows, waves and shells, they can carry for us an emotional charge. Writers who use such natural symbols don't have to inject them with feeling, prime the pump. They need only draw feeling from them, like water from a spring.

Representations of the spiral are characteristic of ancient goddess cultures. Sometimes the spiral is composed of two snakes curled together, one dark, one light, whose heads and eyes are similar to the yin/yang symbol. Two of these spirals are thought to represent the eyes and/or breasts of the goddess; three together may include a third eye and/or womb. At one megalithic cave in Ireland, this symbol at the inner end of the chamber is illuminated by sun on the winter solstice, signaling the return of light at the point of greatest darkness. The snake itself, because it periodically sheds its skin, has been for many ancient cultures a symbol of resurrection. The snake is also equated in India with the life energy or *kundalini* which coils in the pelvis and spirals up through the chakras toward wisdom (B.Walker, 903).

Grahn is clearly playing with this imagery of spiral and snake in her novel. In her down-to-earth terms, Ernesta's mother is a snake charmer, her grandmother Mundane wears the circle of snake teeth around her neck, Mother Ana of the Snake clan of transformation has "one great ancestor snake of changes girdling her waist" (68). Ernesta's world is composed of spiraling realities, all connected. Within this spiral she must learn both bearing and balance.

At the beginning of the novel, the girls, still children, descend into the lower end of the spiral, represented by the root-filled well. At the end they curve with wings above their world. In between they learn from the deaths of two mothers the precariousness of balance. Although death is not viewed in this book as tragic but instead part of the ever returning cycle of life, premature death is a real and not so appealing option. It could possibly be avoided, given the right timing and auspicious fate, if one maintains the right balance between connection and detachment.

When their menstrual blood has begun to flow and they are being initiated into their adulthood, the girls gain the visions that will help them heal the illnesses of their world. These insights emerge from their own individual growth processes, their turning and returning, curving upward, "curling and coiling" (126), dancing and entrancing. Expanding from chamber to chamber, they complete their first full round. Then they can look back on their lives, as if from the top of a spiral staircase, to see how they have evolved from being daughters to becoming potential mothers, capable of "bearing" in all senses of the word.

In keeping with its spiral structure, the novel begins and ends, at different levels of insight, with the same incident. At the beginning, the girls have a limited vision but enough resourcefulness to back in a line out of danger. In the middle of the novel, the girls begin to look back at the mystery of Lillian's death through Ernesta's story telling. At the end they spiral around this incident with a whole different perspective.

The spiral allows for a cyclical pattern without history simply repeating itself. Each time we cycle around an event, we can see it with heightened insight. Now the girls understand not only why Lillian died but also the larger connections: between the earth's energies and the structures we build, between killing and dying, between death and life. They also understand the essential balance between the energies they represent: earth, air, fire and water.

To get to this higher vision, the girls must learn the secrets of transformation, the need to disappear, the simultaneity of loss and gain. They also learn how each one's way is unique. Because of their in-between age, the girls are ripe for transformation. As Ernesta finds out when she plays at healing Jessima and almost chokes her to death, life is no longer just a game. Despite their giggling resistances, they know that "growing up is not too far away" (35).

They learn the connectedness of things, both by exploring on their own the labyrinthian underground system and by observing adults trying to balance and pay heed to mundane realities. They learn their unique talents. Ernesta's "power of transformation [is] based on her wandering eye and subsequent capacity to see on two levels at once" (154); Margedda's wildness and solitude gives her the shamanic ability to die and return; Jessima is sensitive to the structure of things, inner and outer, under and over.

Their uniqueness is affectionately presented through descriptions of their hair: "Ernesta's Head Forms Its Own World"; "Margedda's Hair Is A Beautiful Storm"; Jessima's "spiral coils of fascination." The description of Ernesta's hair is a mundane version of the Hindu mystical vision of the universe:

> Wet, a thousand eyes [like stars] look out... Oiled [it] catches the blue black mineral colors of the world and reflects them

to each other; every hair a mirror for every other... All of it moves in one piece (84).

They learn the final lessons for their transformation from Granmama Mundane, who lives in a basket shaped like a house:

With straw for a house...you stay alert and avid in the dance with transformation, as the snakes do.

She shows them how to make nets so they can learn that:

in a net the spaces are as important throughout as the cord. Space ties everything altogether (158).

One reason Mundane's whole world is healed when the girls experience their initiation together is their insight into how "one creature's line is another's space," something the different clans lost sight of while blaming each other for drought and flood. Entering together the bee-shaped pot, they learn finally the secret of shape shifting. By changing shape, becoming buzzard, cliff, owl, wind and water, they can enter between the lines into all-time and experience visions which will guide their adult lives.

Upon her return from this dream time, Ernesta is given a necklace with one snake fang, the sign of her completion of the first cycle of the spiral of her life:

This is the first day of the first year of your life as a woman... You have shed your childhood skin, and every month you will shed something of your old self and grow something new (190).

In this novel, Grahn fulfills a vision which has been on the feminist agenda since the women's movement was reborn—an initiation for young women, a way of empowerment rather than diminishment as they enter adulthood. She has created an alternative world in which to do this rite of passage. But it's not a fantastic, miraculous world, it's as ordinary and commonplace as our own real lives. Because they dreamed together in the blood ceremony, these girls will be much closer than women in previous generations had been. As "lifelong peers, ruling together," they will know each other's "fragilities and strengths, perspectives and fallings" (190). Although a fictional future, this suggests the bonding which has already taken place in women's communities.

What's remarkable about this book is the tone, playful, childlike, ironic, philosophical. Grahn's lightness of tone suggests a transformation in her style. Always powerful, her voice previously described harsh realities in no uncertain terms, her experience as a battered child, as a working class woman, as a lesbian. With this new lightness she expresses a view from the edge which is neither bitter nor romantic. And from the edge she intuitively realizes a whole world within which communities of women have been healed and out of which another generation of women will be transformed.

Views from the edges are key to what each of these writers shows us about community. Each is in her own way marginal: Walker because she was born poor and Black in a white society and is a revolutionary within the African-American community; Woolf because she was manic-depressive and bisexual; and Grahn because she is working class and lesbian.

First they remind us of the obvious, the inevitability of change, which we are so fond of denying. But then they show us how change is essential to the transformation of communities. Change allows the boundaries of communities to become blurred and permeable, not fixed and closed like the borders of patriarchal inner circles which have traditionally excluded or marginalized so many of us.

Walls break down more readily at the edges than at the solid centers of society. These are places of risk, where little is fixed and safe, where those who have nothing left to lose have most to gain. It is through these spaces in between that the unknown, the new can enter, in the form of a stranger, a long lost relative, a transformed self. Through these cracks, the out can come in, the in can come out, the down can rise up, spirit can find new forms.

Movement, these writers remind us, is essential for growth, and movement comes through the so-called imperfections, the actualities, not the ideals, of our lives, the arrival on the scene of the husband's mistress, the premature death of a hero, a wandering eye. While they acknowledge deaths which occur along with this growth, these writers are even more tuned to the death-in-life that occurs without transformation.

Rejecting the oneness of sameness and stasis, they affirm instead uniqueness and communion. The real bonds between characters occur when people are self-actualized, free to choose, equal. The six in *The Waves* must assert their separate selves, lose their external focus on Percival and face their individual deaths before they can experience a mystical moment of unity. Celie must start fighting back, reject her oppressed status, before she can love herself or forgive Albert. And Mundane's girls must each find her own special power before they can share their common vision quest.

These writers have a reverence for individual entities within larger contexts. This loving attitude generates the unifying spirit of each book. Grounded in the mundane as they are, these visions affirm the imperfection, or uniqueness, of each entity as part of a whole which is itself imperfect, never fully realized, always in the process of growth, death and transformation. Freed from the judging, essentializing and excluding patriarchal alter-ego, women can also be free of that "addiction to perfection" Marion Woodman describes. Perfection assumes a standard set up for all by a few, a norm imposed by the powerful.

As Ursula LeGuin says of *Mundane's World*, what we need in creating our communities are not utopias but these mundane visions, not "blueprints but footprints. Tracks of people going somewhere together" (8). Prints of images, trails of stories are what intuitive process gives us. The symbols which guide these particular journeys are not abstract or absolute but instruments which enable us to sound out the whole of where, for the moment, we are.

CHAPTER TEN

Wider Applications

INTUITIVE INSIGHT has potential for transforming all our activities, from giving birth to dying, from making love to making peace. In fact, since intuition is at least as old as the wheel, there's more need for rediscovery and affirmation than reinvention. Intuition already plays a role in many arenas of our lives, from birthing centers to leave-taking rituals.

In this chapter I will touch upon some fields in which intuition could be or already is particularly fruitful: reproductive rights, drug rehabilitation, health, literacy training, education and women's studies. Since I lack expertise in most of these areas, I offer these comments as seeds which could be planted by those who know more than I do about the soil and climate in which they might grow.

Reproductive Rights

In the sphere of birth control, I offer intuitive method to provide an alternative way of participating in public policy making about reproduction. This process also allows healing within and between participants. The current debate on abortion is so polarized, so tied up in legal and political battles, that real exchange is almost impossible. As Janice Moulton points out in her essay on the adversarial method in philosophy (Harding, 149), this way of discussing issues can result in constricted thinking. As we have seen, it can also be lethal.

From an intuitive perspective, there are many more options and perspectives available than just pro-life and pro-choice. How many people are actually anti-life or anti-choice? How many abortion rights activists believe abortion is the ideal solution? Because it tries to realize the whole, intuition cannot separate the issue of birth control from the fact of birth, the issue of birth from the welfare of both mother and child, the welfare of child and mother from the larger issues of abuse, neglect, childcare, employment, housing and education.

This wider view may sound overwhelming. The complexity of this issue is one reason we feel so helpless in these matters even though our bodies, our lives, our children are at stake. Nevertheless, I wish to sketch out a program for dealing with this complexity that is manageable. This contextual perspective delivers discussion, at least, of the control of reproduction to those who are actually reproducing. This process takes the deliberation out of the hands of "experts," doctors, politicians, judges, most of whom are still men. As biologist Ruth Hubbard points out, leaving these decisions up to lawyers and medical specialists has given us the nonviable situation of fetuses split from wombs, wombs separated from bodies, and children set against their mothers ("Of Embryos and Women," 1).

Rather than buying into the prevailing either/or life versus choice, I call this exploration "Lives and Choices: Giving Birth To and Caring for Our Children and Ourselves." Participants in the discussion would be people either not already polarized or willing to keep their political opinions on hold for awhile. A major effort would be made to include women of all ages, classes, races and ethnic backgrounds, mothers and nonmothers, different sexual preferences, different employments. To encourage participation, ideally a small stipend would be provided for participants' expenses: babysitting, travel, postage, refreshments. Meetings would be held in churches, community centers and possibly homes.

Groups would be formed to allow the greatest amount of diversity possible (including single fathers or househusbands, although I would be inclined to include other men, at least initially, in separate groups to avoid the kind of dominance which has already polarized this debate). This variety might be very difficult at first but would, I believe, be crucial to the intuitive process. Uniformity would defeat the purpose of the groups. Groups would be small (seven is probably the ideal number) and would meet regularly for about a year. Each member would be encouraged to explore (through journal writing and art exercises) and to share her story in relation to the theme of Life and Choices.

These stories would include participants' reproductive history as well as their mothers' and their grandmothers,' and possibly sisters' and brothers.' They might share their experiences as children and the quality of life they have provided or want to provide for their children or child-substitutes (animals included). Participants would be furnished with a series of questions and exercises, and they would be encouraged to modify these or add their own.

My confidence that such a process is not only possible but effective is based on my experience of consciousness-raising and other support groups within the women's movement. The depth of this kind of sharing within my women's studies classes reassures me that it is still a potent process, one that could help bridge the gap between personal experience and public policy.

Questions that emerge would include: What did it feel like to be an unwanted child? an overprotected child? an abused child? a child who must take care of parents or make up for what they didn't have or carry on the family tradition? What was it like to have an unwanted child? to give one up for adoption? to decide to abort? What was it like to be in a large family? to be an only child? to be adopted? to find out you couldn't have children? to be nurtured by non-parents? to be a non-parent taking care of children?

All this, of course, would have to be shared in an atmosphere that is non-judgmental as well as confidential. Guidelines could be suggested for the kinds of responses which would encourage that kind of sharing, and facilitators could assist that process, but even more key would be the kind of intuitive exploration that goes deeper than the verbal, where so many judgments lurk. In the group everyone must be given a chance to explore and share her story, including "if onlys" and "what if I'd made a different choice?" and "if I had to do it over."

After everyone has been heard, the group as a whole would be asked to imagine a story with the following premise: God is about to be born again into this world in the form of a baby girl. Your community, your group, your neighborhood is where she will be born. You might be her mother, her sister, her aunt, her teacher, her neighbor. What kind of life would you choose for her if you could? Imagine this life fully and then describe it by drawing a picture, writing a song or telling her story. In discussing this as a group, what kind of life for her could you all agree on as most fulfilling?

This exercise could then be the basis of sharing between the groups. Each group would tell its version or versions of this myth. This story-telling would be followed by the question, "If you would provide this for the 'greatest' among us, what about the 'least' among us?"

This would provide a transition to related issues of support and education for mothers, employment, health care, the apparent cycle of abuse, childcare and housing. At this point, groups could use intuition to explore connections between these issues. With charts, diagrams and other visual aids, they could draw intuitively upon patterns, continua, processes which emerged from the synthesis of their stories. Each person could also choose a particular issue and make specific recommendations to the whole about that issue.

This process of sharing of stories in a context of non-judgment would allow us to unravel the complex tangle of issues intimately connected to the abortion debate. It might also provide, through the intuitive processes of integration, synthesis and transformation, healing for the traumas related to unwanted pregnancy, abortion, adoption, neglect and abuse. This process would not solve these problems, but it might help us envision new options, new strategies, new values. Such fresh perspectives might be more beneficial to our society than just restricting or providing abortions has been. This process creates a forum within which the people about whom these decisions are being made have a fuller voice in making decisions.

This fuller expression is possible because in fact we are no longer speaking the language of debate and argumentation in which there are winners and losers (which means everyone in some sense loses). We are speaking the language of intuition and art. As John Dewey describes this kind of communication:

> Communication [creates] participation, [makes] common what had been isolated and singular... The expressions that constitute art are communication in its pure and undefiled form. Art breaks through barriers that divide human beings, which are impermeable in ordinary association (244).

One way this process can be taken even deeper is through dream groups or matrices. Sharing our dreams on a regular basis not only allows us to know each other more profoundly, it also allows us to dream together, to envision a shared future and to understand more fully our larger world. Lawrence's descriptions of "social dreaming" among the Aborigines of Taiwan and the Senoi of the Malay Peninsula, as well as contemporary Israelis and Germans, reveal how meaningful and moving the sharing of dreams can be, uncovering the hidden agendas, repressions and visions which propel so many global events.

Given that most of us won't have the luxury of participating in such a full process, we can still apply this intuitive method to our various interactions, on the job, at meetings, in groups. Whenever the discussion threatens to turn into a heated debate or a polarized standstill, each person can be asked to drop into her or his own experience and connect that to the position she or he feels so strongly about. Understanding a person's background, context and personal experience will allow for a greater diversity of views and might open up some new alternatives. Whenever there is strong feeling combined with intolerance or misunderstanding, the participants can try to share, with non-verbal as well as verbal modes, connections between convictions, feelings and experience.

Such processing may seem like a detour from the task at hand, but it can help us out of (or to avoid) the dead end of deadlocked argument. It also has potential for releasing us from the grip of categorical thinking, the bodyguard of stereotyping judgment, without erasing distinctions essential to understanding differences. Telling a story about how a particular person in a particular context abused or discriminated against us can, I believe, help us avoid judging a whole category of people with which the abuser or discriminator can be identified. Expressing our anger and hurt this way can defuse the need to globalize our repressed or unvalidated negative emotion with racial, class, ethnic or gender generalizations. Such sharing will not solve the problem of habitual xenophobia, people projecting their negative qualities onto others/strangers, like racists who've never known a Black person. But it will free up more space between people who are trying to get to know each other.

A deeper understanding by each person and of each person can result from this processing, an understanding which facilitates further interaction and decision making. Sometimes a synthesis of points of view creates a new position for some. Sometimes this sharing creates a new perspective for the whole group. Sometimes it moves one or all to action that was not foreseen until the sharing. It affects not just who we are together but what we do together.

Drug Rehabilitation

Since the widespread use of drugs is caused by multiple factors, the most serious of which are economic and racial discrimination, intuition in itself cannot effect any changes in this area. But it can help those in treatment programs find a cure, and if used more in education it might have some preventive power.

Interviews with adolescent marijuana users reveal that what they claim to receive from smoking is the kind of experience (mystical insight, musical sensitivity, contact with metaphoric or symbolic realities) lacking in much of their education. In schools arts are too often relegated to minimal or elite status, and imagination is sometimes regarded as spacey, impractical or unprofitable.

Stanislav Grof's theory, based on insights from William James and C.G. Jung about alcoholism, is that substance abuse is compensation for unmet spiritual needs. The epidemic use of drugs among teenagers can also be seen as an attempt to self-medicate for the powerlessness, stress, joblessness and shrinking opportunities in their lives.

The materialistic values of the 80's echoed the suffocating values of the 50's which drove many artists and spiritual seekers to drug-use in the 60's. This provides an ironic counterpart to the economic deprivation and despair which has steered so many poor people toward drug use decade after decade. Whether the problem is too much or too little, an obsession with material well-being can trigger a need for the spiritual transcendence which drugs promise.

Drug use is not just symptomatic. It is an attempt to self-cure, to provide what is lacking. What people need, young and old both, are alternatives, challenges that call forth their imagination and creativity, as well as their effectiveness, thoughtfulness and emotional sensitivity. If we provide a nurturing ground for children's natural intuitive abilities during their "magical years," we will have a headstart on preventing drug abuse as well as discouraging social passivity, alienation and vulnerability to exploitation.

For many young people whose emotions are so strong and whose families can't listen, intuitive expression through the arts might provide both an outlet and an audience for their feelings. Susanne Langer's description of the education of feeling through art is inspiring in this regard:

> Artistic training is...the education of feeling, as our schooling [in facts and logic]...is the education of thought. Few people realize that the real education of emotion is not "conditioning"...but tacit, personal, illuminating contact with symbols of feeling (*FAF*, 409).

A transfusion of intuitive training into our educational systems will give more joy, meaning, play and insight to the lives of teenagers and adults as well. Intuitive training for teachers will enable us to recognize and tap into our students' capacity for growth and to help them realize their potential.

I am intrigued with how intuition is being used in actual drug treatment programs. The use of artistic imagination seems to me not just a way to detox but also a way to discover an alternative to drug-induced visions. But how to integrate this kind of exploration with the other needs of a person who is trying to change self-destructive habits? The answer to this question is being discovered by healers who are actually working in this field. The dimension of story telling is already a key ingredient in A.A. and other recovery programs. Expressive arts therapies have proven enormously creative and useful for addiction problems as well as the traumas behind them. More of this work, like David Oldfield's work on mythic journeys with hospitalized adolescents (Peay, 7), can be integrated into places like schools and community centers which touch the lives of ordinary people.

Health

Recently I saw a film of the interior of a living human body with views of the heart pumping, the veins pulsing, the lungs breathing (IMAX's "To the Limit"). Although I have often imagined what was going on inside my physical being, this perspective changed how I think about my body, as well as how I treat it. Since I've seen from the inside, I've become a lot healthier. Analogously, a person who is encouraged to drop into her or his inner self and explore it through intuition has, as a result of that fuller perspective, a better chance of becoming emotionally, spiritually and physically healthier.

The area of health is one where intuitive practice has already been developed to a sophisticated degree. Although the medical establishment is still resistant to anything not based on empirical evidence, alternative medicine with a wholistic approach has been flourishing. Much of what I've learned about intuition's power to heal, or make whole again, in addition to my own creative work, has come from experiences with some of these wholistic practices: psychosynthesis, guided imagery, expressive arts, dreambody work and rebirthing. Dialogue with practitioners in these field has also been instructive. I am particularly grateful to my sister Ann, who as a counselor was a pioneer explorer of alternative therapies long before they became popular, and to my friend Maria Courie, who introduced me to her own intuitive blend of alternative techniques at crucial junctures in my own search.

Translating some of this knowledge into teaching, I have been impressed with how, given opportunity and tools, adults in my intuition class have been able, on their own, with little actual class time or guidance from me, to heal themselves, solve problems, discover personal transformations. My own experience of alternative therapies, plus the experience of facilitating workshops on personal growth through the arts, has given me confidence to provide this opportunity. Having done so, I realize intuition provides the crucial ingredient of nurturing people's faith in their own healing powers.

One area where this source of faith could probably be explored even further is in nursing education. So many of my students and friends who are nurses or in other medical fields have remarked how useful it has been for them to receive confirmation of their intuitive abilities. In their work, although they frequently rely on these abilities, in a medical setting they have to hide or apologize for them. The more they can trust their own intuition, the more they can challenge doctors about diagnosis and treatment and the more they can assist patients whose care is mostly in their hands.

Literacy Training

Judging from the latest National Report Card, illiteracy threatens to become an even greater problem than it already is. From discussions with friends who are experts in this area, I realize how complex an issue this is, so I won't presume to offer an intuitive method as a solution. Instead I'll just suggest how intuition might contribute.

As my work with the neighborhood children showed me, a problem with language skills does not reveal a lack of imagination or story telling ability. As the new research on the brain suggests, the intelligence of the frontal lobe, while it might be engaged in very insightful inner speech, has no direct motor connection to the part of the brain which produces discursive language. Contrary to what many of us composition teachers have believed, language may not be the essence of thought.

Unfortunately for many students, some teachers are more interested in logic, spelling and grammar than in listening to their stories. But where there is emotional sensitivity and imagination, intuition flourishes. That in turn provides motivation for wanting to develop more sophisticated communication skills. Once people are connected to their own deepest feelings and can find imaginative, symbolic expression for these feelings, they will obviously be more willing to struggle with language problems than if they are passively responding to given materials or performing rote drills. This seems to be as true for adults as for children. Once they make the connection, however, adults may be more willing to stick to the drills than children are.

This emotional/imaginative base is even more crucial for the many Americans who don't grow up speaking standard English. What intuition allows is a healing of the language, making it whole again—so that expression can come not just through words, statements and grammar, but with tone of voice and gesture and symbol as well. The trauma of migration/assimilation, which most Americans have either experienced or inherited, has resulted in a splitting of the language. Not only have people been separated from their native tongues in terms of words, they are also split from those innate sounds, images and body language. What exists for them as Standard English are words and statements devoid of the other elements which make language whole. Anthropological studies indicate that for ancient peoples art, music, drama and ritual were part of one unified expression. Language training which integrates the expressive arts might create a context in which people could learn more easily to read and to write.

Education

Understanding how intuition works has deep implications for education on numerous levels. It can help us understand cultures outside the dominant Western tradition which, despite vast differences among them, rely greatly on intuitive perception. Studies of these cultures therefore have much to teach us about intuition. What we learn can be used to create curricula more supportive of students rooted in these other cultures. With these materials we can meet people where they are, affirm them as well as expand their and our ways of learning. Understanding intuition can also give teachers greater access to students whose learning styles are personally more intuitive than rational.

Intuition is crucial to multicultural education. It can help create a synthesis for a new American language that is unified without being uniform. Whenever there is cultural diversity untainted by prejudice and judgments about correctness, people borrow from each other, imitate each other, exchange forms of communication. Away from the media with its norm of "white bread" spread from a buffet of stereotypes, we do learn from each other. On common ground, the shared context of our present lives, we can appreciate what different roots have produced: gestures, words, tones, images and perspectives which express certain realities more fully than our own dialect can.

Already our language is richer for the infusion of such modes of expression as African-American gestures of salutation or the use of "be" for the abiding present; words like *mensch* or *tush*, along with Yiddish intonations; the precision of Italian-American gestures; Irish-American lyricism; Japanese-American movement and ritual; words like *machismo, chi, karma*. All these have become part of our popular lingo.

But imagine what richness we could share if even deeper roots of various cultures were tapped into so they could be taught in our schools as part of *our* language and culture study. Not just Chinese sayings from fortune cookies, but quotes from *The Tao*. Not just lox and bagels but the rituals blessing Jewish passages. Not just belly dances but Sufi wisdom. Not just madras bedspreads but meditation practice. Not just Native American pottery but spiritual visions. Not just afros but African mythology and culture. Not just burritos but magical realism.

This country is already rich in cultural diversity, but so impoverished by how shallow our sharing is. Allowing more intuitive play into the study of language, the language we really speak in all its facets, would not only nourish communication between us, but also enrich our appreciation for our shared cultures.

To carve out more space for such a context of sharing, we also need to be more creative with the metaphors we use for multicultural identity. The melting pot image clearly doesn't appeal to those who do not wish to assimilate to the extent that they lose their identities in the stew of American oneness. The salad, with its variety of uncooked tastes, blended but not merged, offers a more appetizing analogy in this health conscious age. Given the diversity of culinary offerings which can be found today in most large cities, one might wish for something even more mouth-watering: an international banquet.

But are food imagery and consumption really the most effective ways to symbolize what we hope for in the fullest flowering of democracy? What other metaphors might express that diversity-in-unity which for many of us would be the true fulfillment of the American dream? What image can maneuver us between the conformity and chaos feared by partisans on either side of the multicultural debate?

My own intuitive vision for multicultural education is a network of mini United Nations. The model is based on my experiences with the international Grail. To avoid the limitations of identity politics or the potential domination of ethnic majorities, we need meeting places where people representative of varying backgrounds can voluntarily come together as potential equals (acknowledging the inequalities of class divisions which could not be relieved by this system). To avoid potential power imbalances, no one background would have more representatives than another. Groups would be small enough to allow the kind of sharing described for the Lives and Choices group. The process of sharing would also include the full spectrum of artistic and intuitive communication. Given existing demographics, these encounters could only happen under temporary circumstances which allow people to travel to some neutral common ground without having to give up their home bases. Summer camps, retreat centers and adult education centers offer possible sites. Funding and accreditation would have to be provided to allow people with differing resources to participate.

Current trends in the women's community toward recognizing cultural diversity and encouraging its expression, in elementary schools toward whole language, experiential and hands-on learning, in universities toward interdisciplinary and multicultural programs, and in language and ESL learning toward contextual, immersion, wholistic approaches offer supportive matrices for intuitive education.

As a teacher in a non-traditional program, I see intuition as essential to the interdisciplinary study we encourage. It allows an organic growth of a student's exploration of a key question, issue, problem or theme across disciplinary boundaries. It also provides a symbolic language by which expanding insights can be expressed. The question remains how to integrate intuitive language and process more explicitly into the core of such study. While I believe that intuition should be taught, along with critical thinking, as a fundamental tool for non-traditional education, I am also struck by the incongruity of intuition wearing the uniform of a required course.

Some would claim that intuition is so idiosyncratic it cannot be taught. This may be true if we define teaching in a traditional sense, with its emphasis on control, content, expertise and discipline. But I know from the experience of teaching courses and workshops on creativity that intuitive language and process can be learned, even while the event of intuition remains mysterious and unpredictable. Intuitive language springs forth in children like bean plants, and even in repressed adults, after some focused mining, it can emerge like veins of precious ore. The key to integrating intuition into both traditional and non-traditional programs is, I believe, trusting the intuition of teachers in these programs.

Intuitive training for teachers at all levels of education would also be helpful. Its purpose would not be to teach them anything new, but, as with the nurses, to encourage them to value and trust their own intuitive approaches. My sister Mary is a bilingual kindergarten teacher in San Antonio, Texas. Watching a tape of her classroom, I was impressed with how intuitive her teaching is. A study which identified and encouraged such intuitive methodology would not only serve the teachers involved but, through them, other educators as well.

More intuitive education also has the potential for responding to the fragmentation and alienation which play such forceful roles in current national crises. The ability to see things whole which intuition provides could be an important springboard for students' gaining insight into such diverse issues as ecological disaster, economic imbalances and splits between racial and ethnic groups. Children can learn to trust their intuitive ability to realize the connections between parts of themselves, between themselves and others, between the self and the world, and to see the potential consequences inherent in their actions. These insights will give them opportunities to advance beyond the self-absorption, short sightedness and tunnel vision of prevailing systems. Although fragmentation and alienation are nothing new in our world, these problems are reaching a crisis point. So much evil in our world has already resulted from cutting off of one part of the whole (the human community, nature, the cosmos) from another: holocaust, apartheid, ethnic cleansing and abuse of groups and classes of people—particularly of women and children, of animals and of the environment.

Recognizing intuition as one learning style natural to many children is part of the movement within feminist pedagogy/andragogy and within non-traditional education which acknowledges diverse ways of knowing. Intuition is obviously only one of many ways. It's no more important than emotional or visual or relational or hands-on learning. But intuition itself assures us that allowing as much diversity as possible will provide the best education for the most students. It will also give us the fullest reservoir of knowledge and knowers for the future.

Women's Studies

While we are helping others grow intuitively, we can use intuition to critique present day institutions and their oppressively gendered metaphors, their "seminal" ideas and "penetrating" insights. At the same time we women can rely on intuition for symbolic transformations which can help move us forward.

For example, there is much talk in women's studies these days about "margins" and "the center." The metaphor of "marginal" originates with patriarchal texts which have so excluded us that we have had to write ourselves into the margins. Combined with the image of "the center," the margin analogy also suggests a circle which includes the privileged and excludes us: "They drew a circle and left me out." This flat concentric world looks like a pie. If everyone got an equal share of this American pie, then each piece would contain a wedge of the center and a juicy portion of margin.

But even served up as democratic socialism, this image is really too static a symbol to describe the transformation which is now taking place between those considered marginal and those in power. Once we question from whose point of view experience is judged central, then, as Elizabeth Minnich puts it, "what we are doing is as radical as undoing geocentricism, the notion that the earth is the center of the cosmos" (14).

Symbolically, jumping back further into world history, we can no longer believe that the earth is flat. Once the earth rounds herself, our world is much larger than a page in a book written neither by nor about us. It's fuller than a pie we can't eat (even when we are expected to bake it).

Viewing the earth as a globe, we begin to ask different questions about margins and centers. None of us humans, however powerful and privileged, could survive at the center, the core. On the surfaces, or edges, where we all live, the earth has many different centers. There are centers of stability which shift with the tides, centers of fertility which shift with the sun, centers of prosperity which shift with the stars, centers of power which shift with the human story and centers of wisdom which deepen and dissolve in ways which can't be charted.

Symbolic transformation can shift our language and our thought as radically as the realization that the earth is a sphere revolutionized exploration. No doubt both science and poetry can provide us with more dynamic images for the changes we are making and experiencing in our lives and in our institutions. Nature herself offers ample opportunity for observing how the edges and the cores of things are continually exchanging forms, dissolving into one another, generating new energy and new structures for this energy. Such symbols, brought into fuller consciousness by the stories which emerge from them, can, in turn, guide us toward deeper transformations of our language and our action.

Intuition alone cannot root out the sources of greed, prejudice, fear and hostility which lie at the base of some of these issues. Intuition must be combined with our other powers to facilitate effective actions, particularly actions to heal and transform our society. But by contributing a more harmonious instrument with which to sound out these issues, intuition may well supply a crucial missing piece.

Part Three
THEORIES ABOUT INTUITION

CHAPTER ELEVEN

What is "Women's Intuition"?

> Nice Guy Seeks...
> Earthy, sensitive, intuitive whole lady,
> under 40...
> (*Gnosis*, 1989)

I CAN'T help wondering if this nice guy is searching for his other half, someone who will compensate for his abstract, insensitive, rational, fragmentary, aging self. Or is he himself just as earthy, sensitive, intuitive and whole? The relevant question here, however, is what he means by intuition, or more importantly how the lady herself, should she materialize, defines her intuitiveness.

Three distinct associations come to mind when we talk about women's intuition. One is instinct, one is wariness and one is authority through an inner voice. Instinct is often called "gut-level intuition." Although guts are not gender-specific, one New Age woman associates this basic visceral feeling with the female:

> Since a woman's womb is at the second chakra [the center of gut-level intuition] it may explain why this is often called "women's intuition" (Gardner, 65).

The second association is the wariness of the oppressed, the survival traits of being able to read between the lines, sense what is about to happen, second-guess the bosses. As Jean Baker Miller describes these traits:

> Subordinates...become highly tuned to the dominants... Here... is where the long story of "feminine intuition" and "feminine wiles" begins.... These mysterious gifts are in fact skills,

developed through long practice, in reading many small signals (10).

The third association with women's intuition is the inner authority developed by women who have been denied access to external sources like education or to positions of power within patriarchal hierarchies. This use of the inner voice by mystics like Hildegarde of Bingen, artists like Emily Dickenson and activists like Sojourner Truth is documented by Gerda Lerner in *The Creation of Feminist Consciousness*. Whether or not this inner authority was called intuition by the women who drew upon it, popular references to intuition, particularly by women, assume this meaning.

There is no doubt that historically all of these different kinds of knowing have been practiced by women. But are they necessarily intuition? And is there anything essentially female about them? Men may not have wombs, but they have visceral instincts. Subordinate men or those denied authority by reasons of race, class or other forms of discrimination have also developed sixth senses and inner voices for survival and growth.

But the real problem with trying to pin down what we mean when we speak of "women's intuition" is that the social construction of *Woman* is currently being dismantled piece by piece. Every impulse, habit and gene is under scrutiny for its gender identity. Considerations of race, ethnicity, class, age and sexual preference raise deeper questions about what we mean by the term *woman*. Combined with the already slippery term *intuition*, it's not clear when we speak of *women's intuition*, whether the ground we stand on is rock, mud or quicksand.

However, many of us, either through socialization or self-identification, still to some extent inhabit the old constructs. Having remodeled them more to our liking, we women have scraped away the misogynist crust around legacies like intuition and may even be ready to claim them. As one of my students put it, "I'm glad intuition belongs to women. I like having it tacked on to my status."

We may still need to search through the attic or cellar of the old construct of *Woman* for clues about our intuitive inheritance. Like vintage clothing these remnants might not show us much about our contemporary gender identities, but they may yield hints about some features of intuition which have been devalued just because they were assigned in a derogatory manner to women.

The question of whether there is a woman's intuition, different from men's, is dealt with by two contemporary writers on intuition, Frances Vaughn and Philip Goldberg. Since one is a woman and the other a man, we can find in the titles of their books reflections of their generalizations about gender: *Awakening Intuition* and *The Intuitive Edge.*

"Awakening" suggests a mother waking a child. "Edge" implies sharpness, a sword, adventure (play the edges, journey to the edges of the world). Awakening is personal, a voice calling, a touch. Edge means knowledge, getting ahead, competition, pushing boundaries. In their discussions Vaughn is more relational, interested in making connections and Goldberg more objective, interested in making distinctions. She seems to speak from inside her experience of intuition, sometimes blurring distinctions between it and other kinds of knowing (psychic, mystical). He seems so far outside of it, analyzing, talking about it, that I sometimes wondered if he'd actually experienced it.

For Frances Vaughn, what is called *women's intuition* is the emotional level of intuition. She cites research by Judith Hall showing women's greater sensitivity to non-verbal communication. She then associates an "expanded awareness of the emotional level...with an increase in synchronicity and psychic experiences" (71). She concludes:

> There is no evidence that women are inherently different in their intuitive capacities, but the popular belief that women are more intuitive is related to the fact that women in our society are not taught to repress feelings as much as men (70).

Goldberg's analysis of "the folklore of feminine intuition" is similarly inconclusive. He cites studies which suggest that men test better on spatial visualization and geometry but focus more narrowly when problem-solving and that women are more sensitive to context and process information more quickly, characteristics which can relate to intuitive procedure. He points out that these differences are not absolute but averages and that on a continuum, differences within each gender are wider than between the sexes. He concludes:

> On the whole, behavioral tests provide no evidence for women's intuition; at best they constitute a partial explanation if the phenomenon exists (95).

Even though Goldberg dismisses ideas that the hemispheres of the brain can be assigned to different genders or that intuition resides in the right half, he is intrigued by evidence which suggests that women have a greater ability to switch from one hemisphere to the other while men specialize more:

> If, as I suspect, intuition involves a kind of hemispheric synchrony, this might support the idea that women are more intuitive. But that, too, is conjecture (96).

What he refers to here corresponds to what Anne Bowbeer describes, in relation to the *corpus callosum* which connects the cerebral hemispheres, as "hemispheric lateralization of male brains and integration of the hemispheres of female brains." Evidence for this conclusion is based on electroencephalograph readings, biofeedback studies, damaged brain research and tests of tactile and auditory perception. These studies, she claims, point toward men being specialists and women generalists (9). Feminist scientists like Anne Fausto-Sterling have criticized the limited data on which these conclusions are based.

Goldberg also describes reasons men resist being labeled intuitive: cultural conditioning which judges logic superior and makes men avoid the emotionalism, fantasy and spaciness associated with both intuition and the feminine; male pride, "being in charge," which requires control and objectivity.

He skates on thin ice when he argues that social conditioning toward passivity makes women more open to intuition, which "comes most readily to a receptive, patient mind, one that yields to it." Equating a forced passivity with a creative receptivity seems to romanticize oppression. Dismissing women's rationality while affirming their emotional sensitivity seems problematic as well:

> Women have not been discouraged from having feelings, either the emotional kind or the cognitive kind. Until they enter traditional masculine domains, they have less motivation to be analytic and objective and less need to argue logically (97).

With little patience or passivity, many feminists have resisted this assignment to the emotional pole of cognition. They have used their own analyses to argue against traditional male rattling of the weapon of reason. Daly described such use as "gang rape of women's minds"; De Beauvoir called masculine logic "a form of violence"; Cixous drew analogies between the male brain and the male sex organ: "linear, hard, penetrating but impenetrable"; Harding portrayed male rationality as "tough, rigorous, impersonal, competitive, unemotional, objectifying [and] inextricably intertwined with separation and individuation" (Hawkesworth, 540); and LeGuin characterized "the Father Tongue" as lecturing, dichotomizing, distancing, talking down and not listening.

LeGuin, however, was careful not to equate reasoning itself with the use made of it within patriarchy. All these thinkers were counter-attacking the dichotomy of thought into binary oppositions (object/subject, head/heart, rational/intuitive, culture/nature, male/female) which have been wielded hierarchically to subordinate women and other people.

In doing so, however, these feminists have treaded close to the trap of themselves gendering reason. Women's supposedly more intuitive, contextual, connected and caring way of knowing becomes the superior pole. Turning the hierarchy upside down does not necessarily free us from the either/or constrictions of dichotomized thinking. Even the categories of masculine and feminine used skillfully by Jungian feminists like Marion Woodman to describe qualities found in both women and men tend to reinforce old stereotypes. While these terms are crucial tools for plumbing the depths of our transitional consciousness, they can still lock us into old and stultifying forms.

These counter-attacks over the turf of reason are invigorating and self-affirming. Fighting back is an important stage of development for us as women. Stopping at the plateau of what Judith Newton calls "comic essentialism," however, can be a delusion. As Hawkesworth observes:

> Given the diversity and fallibility of all human knowers, there is no good reason to believe that women are any less prone to error, deception or distortion than men (544).

It can even be dangerous to indulge too fully in a self-glorification which, according to Nina Auerbach:

> purges women of all violence and ego until we become a gush of sheer nurturance in an angry world... When [we] attribute

all aggression...to men alone, [we give our] own potential violence to [our] oppressor, making him more loomingly omnipotent than any actual man (Benstock, 150).

Defusing these polarized categories continues to be a critical and liberating operation. Clearly intuition has been projected by Eurocentric men on to women because they devalued it in themselves, yet recognized it might be useful to have around the house. I remain curious, however, whether there has been something in the historical conditions of being a woman which actually fostered intuition.

Take, for instance, the circumstance of being a housewife. Although this never was an isolated option for all women (those who were unmarried or who had to work to support their families), did being a housewife necessitate being intuitive? Housewives at their best see everything at once, take care of everybody at the same time, know their homes contextually. Do men who are now house-husbands find their consciousnesses becoming more intuitive—less focused, more tuned to peripheral input? Are working mothers, playing both roles, even more intuitive? Or are we all just too busy these days to bother with intuitive reception or expansion?

Having mulled over this question of women's intuition, I have located three areas where traditional gender difference might contribute to different kinds of intuitive realization. They are: 1. experience and consciousness of the time/space continuum; 2. the connection of emotion to intuition; and 3. permeable boundaries between self and other.

Space and Time

Do men and women experience space and time differently? Is there, as Elaine Showalter suggests, a "woman's time, woman's space"? Or are women space and men time, as Blake suggests?

One of the clearest most convincing descriptions of such a gender distinction can be found in Mary O'Brien's *The Politics of Reproduction:* For women, "The female reproductive consciousness is a universal consciousness, common to all women" (50). A midwife/philosopher, O'Brien is able to distinguish uniquely female experience without falling into old stereotypes (a danger Elizabeth Davis, also a midwife, in her *Women's Intuition* does not avoid).

According to O'Brien:

> [pregnancy and menstruation] are the visible and communally understood signs of female potency, of the unity of potential and actual. All women carry the consciousness of this unity, just as all women carry the notion of suffering, labor and decisions to [make] (50).

Men, on the other hand:

> are separated by the alienation of the seed from continuity over time. There is no tangible, experiential link between generations, no mediation of the time gap as women experience... Female time is continuous, while male time is discontinuous (52).

(For further exploration of O'Brien's thesis see *Taking Our Time: Feminist Perspectives on Temporality*.)

Jung's description of the intuitive person raises further questions about gender differences in relation to time and space:

> Only through envisioning possibilities is intuition fully satisfied... When it is the dominant function, every ordinary situation in life seems like a locked room which intuition has to open... Because he is always seeking out new possibilities, stable conditions suffocate him. (*The Portable Jung*, 260).

The generic "he" here is not accidental. What Jung describes is a masculine, at least one man's, experience of time/space. The metaphors of locked doors, suffocation, tearing down walls are telling. The new is always something out there, beyond the confines of the present moment which is symbolized by domestic security. It is something one moves out to, progresses towards, consumes or uses and then moves on from. The new is something one is born to or something one "penetrates" (another term Jung uses for intuitive vision) and then leaves behind.

From a woman's perspective, the new is, or can be, not just something we are born to, but also, whether or not we are biological mothers, something to which we give birth. With periodic reminders of our fertility most women experience the potential of time fulfilling itself within us. We don't have to go anywhere else to know about the expanding moment which starts from practically nothing and expands, issuing monthly as blood or, after a wider cycle of time, emerging as a child.

But women are not the only people whose inner space, whether empty or full, can tune to intuitive time or kairos. The intuitive moment, if we allow it, can expand within any of us and resonate out into cycles of nature and the seasons, spirals of personal and communal growth. Anyone outside of the treadmill of modern society can feel this kind of time: native peoples, farmers, old people, children, those who are ill, those who are meditating, those who are artists, those who are poor, those who are shamans or medicine people. Only those who are run by the clock or busy climbing the success pyramid, women as well as men, find that time and space are outside them. For them what is new must be pursued across great distances while at their backs they "always hear time's winged chariot hurrying near" (Marvell). In that truncated space there is of necessity a greater separation of self and experience.

Female or male, most people in industrialized societies are cut off from the ancient intuitive experiences of time symbolized by the yin/yang, the spiral, the wheel, the tree of life, to the extent that they are severed from nature and her cycles. It has taken us more than a century to realize the cost, pollution, exhaustion, spiritual poverty, we've paid for ignoring that fuller vision while chasing the latest possibility for forward movement which we call progress around the next bend.

Our sense of interior time is only a memory of what it's like to live out of doors with nature's balance of day and night, dawn and dusk. Most Americans cling to the business of daylight and shun the dangers of night, allowing ourselves little of its comfort, its richness of shadows, fireflies, animal calls, stars, moon, northern lights. Night has become a time to shrink inside our selves. For women "taking back the night" (originally, a political march for women's safety in the streets) is crucial not only for protection and freedom of movement but also for an expansion of that intuitive sense of time we carry within.

Emotion

Because of the vital connection between emotion and intuition, being able to tune-in to our feelings is an integral preparation for intuition. Dewey describes emotion as "the moving and cementing force" which gives one unifying color to the disparate parts of an experience (42). Jung describes how symbols are "integrally connected to the living individual by the bridge of the emotions" (*MHS*,

90). Some people value intuition yet dismiss the importance of emotion, without realizing the vital link between intuitive insight and emotion, without recognizing emotion's crucial role in unifying perceptions and energizing symbols.

Given this connection, the question is, are women, as traditionally socialized, more emotional than men, and therefore more intuitive? Many gender theorists claim that women are allowed and encouraged to be more tuned to their own and other's emotions than men are. This is not to say that women are actually more sensitive or more expressive. Men in many cultures, for example, are generally permitted expression of anger more easily than most women.

Ethnographic studies suggest, in fact, that emotion is socially constructed, not universal, natural, raw feeling (Lutz). Consequently, cultural conditions must be taken into consideration when estimating the extent to which emotions are conditioned by gender. In Muslim and Mediterranean cultures emotions like grief, which are considered weak, are thrust upon women who are also considered weak. Expressing such emotions is taboo for men who learn, instead, to express feelings like anger (Grima, 11). In cultures where women are required to be the major breadwinners, emotionality might be an indulgence the breadwinner cannot afford. In any survival situation, war, genocide, famine, disaster, emotional expression, even lamentation, often must be put on hold. Public display of emotion, unless highly ritualized, is still frowned upon in many patriarchal societies. The more women join the public arena, the less emotional they may become. As Benedicte Grima points out in her study of Paxtun women, even the concept of personal or private feeling is a cultural construct (8).

It has been argued that mothering duties allow or require women to be more emotional. Those whose primary responsibility is caring for children are expected to be sensitive to the emotions of the children. Not all caretakers actually are, as indicated by widespread child abuse and the thriving therapy business. Those who are sensitive to the feelings of others may be so at the expense of knowing what their own feelings are, as the epidemic of co-dependency indicates.

While emotional awareness can generate intuitive insight, it does not guarantee effective intuitive expression. No matter how emotional an individual may be to begin with, as she tries to communicate her insights, she will discover the difference between the catharsis of pure emotional self-expression and the symbolic transformation of feeling which occurs when expressive forms are fully articulate:

Artistic utterance strives to create as complete and transparent a symbol as possible, whereas personal utterance, under the stress of actual emotion, usually contents itself with half-articulated symbols, just enough to explain the symptoms of inner pressure (Langer, *FAF*,139).

Intuition also evokes other feelings, called aesthetic emotions, which are not necessarily influenced by gender socialization toward sensitivity or expressiveness. These feelings of awe, joy and fulfillment accompany intuitive realization and expression. Any discoverer, whether artist, scientist or explorer, can feel them. Biologist Barbara McClintock describes her experience:

Not that I had the answer but I had the joy of going at it. When you have that joy, you do the right experiments. You let the material tell you where to go...with an overall brand new pattern in mind (125).

Permeable Boundaries

A third area of alleged gender difference where insights into intuitive process might be mined is the theory that women have more permeable boundaries between self and other than men do. If this is true, they would be more open to intuitive insight which leaps the gap between knower and known. Women would be more empathetic, more willing to identify with others, and this, we have seen, is one of the primary steps in the intuitive process.

This theory about boundaries is based on Nancy Chodorow's hypothesis that because of different relationships with their mothers, females have more fluid ego boundaries. As a result:

Girls come to experience themselves as less differentiated than boys, as more continuous with and related to the external object-world (167).

Some feminists interpret this permeable boundary as negative, a failure "to separate from their mothers because their mothers failed to separate from them" (Baym, 53). Others celebrate a receptive feminine consciousness.

In describing this fluidity of borders between self and other, Sylvia Perera recognizes the double-sidedness of such merger in its blissful union and in the loss of individual autonomy. The unbounded zone allows expansion of consciousness, but it also threatens to swallow up the separate self.

If it is true that mothers and daughters experience this lack of differentiation, it may be because they are both female or because they inherit the same socialized role. In either case, an assumed resulting ability to identify would assist women to be more intuitive only up to a certain point. Identification is only one part of the intuitive process.

By many accounts, intuition is also accompanied by a certain detachment. The I-Thou configuration, in other words, must be balanced by a corresponding "disidentification." This paradoxical quality of intuitive empathy is described by Frances Vaughn in distinguishing identification from projection or fantasy. Such impartiality requires both "control of the mind and surrender of the egotistical will" (31).

Other writers refer to this state of involved detachment as psychic or aesthetic distance or disinterest. It is not the cold, aloof separating of self we associate with objectivity but such full participation that the grasping, opportunistic ego is momentarily suspended:

> Distance is a name for a participation so intimate and balanced that no particular impulse acts to make a person withdraw, a completeness of surrender in perception (Dewey, 258).

This intense contemplation is obviously not inherent in either male or female socialization.

These three areas of possible gender differentiation do open windows to a deeper understanding of the intuitive process. They don't, however, prove that women are more intuitive than men. They can suggest some ways women's intuition might be different. Women might have a more grounded experience of inner space and time, they might have access to a broader spectrum of emotional expression, and they might be more empathic. These qualities would give them easier access to some stages of the intuitive process but not necessarily other stages. And chances are impossible that such generalizations would be true of all women of different ethnic backgrounds, classes, races, lifestyles and abilities—even before what we know as the historical reality of Woman is eventually deconstructed. Better that we realize intuition as a capacity we humans could all afford to develop more fully, whatever future studies of the brain might reveal about gender differences.

What ultimately bothers me about the idea of women's intuition is that the gendering of intuition in itself is not intuitive but a construct of rational dualistic thinking. Intuition is more interested in intensity, variety and depth of experience, wherever it resides, than in comparing and measuring types of people. Such abstract dichotomizing and polarizing is totally unintuitive. Intuition would see femininity and masculinity as multiple points on a continuum occupied by various actual women and men. And it would be more interested in the particularities of their individual lives than in generalizations.

As an activity, intuition connects unique individual experience with larger, expanding wholes. Important as group identity can be, intuition is more interested in how that identity is experienced personally. The intuitive route allows us to tell our stories whether we're representative of an oppressed category (poor, lesbian, woman of color) or an oppressive category (white, middle class, educated) or, often, some unique mix of both. What matters intuitively is what happens between categories of identity, how those conditions create consciousness, the mysterious chemistry of each person's special combination of traits and identities. Intuition reminds us, through their poetry, that no one African-American, lesbian, single mother, poet is exactly like another African-American, lesbian, single mother, poet.

Whether there is such a phenomenon as women's intuition, it is clear from the voices we have heard through this book—girls, students, artists, philosophers, psychologists and scientists—that, no matter what each says intuition is, the intuitions of women are thriving.

In fact, women's intuitions have thrived for millennia, surviving genocide, rape, poverty and war. Fruits of their intuitions, thank the goddesses, are finally being rediscovered.

I made my dress with help from my mother and grandmother. I borrowed colors from the natural world...floral pattern from my sisters the flowers. When I wear my soft, doeskin dress the spirit of the deer will always be with me (Thom, 9).

CHAPTER TWELVE

Mapping Some Distinctions

The term "intuition" is one of the most ambiguous in the whole range of thought (Dewey, 294).

[Intuition is] a slough of despond for the philosopher (Langer, *PNK* 85).

"Intuition" has been used by philosophers to designate many things—some of which are suspicious characters (Dewey, 192).

AS YOUR guide into this sphere of intuition, I would like to leave you with a map which helps define the larger territory in which intuition is located. In exploring its dimensions, I don't plan to plot its boundaries with precision, and I certainly don't intend to raise fences between it and other experiences with which it is often equated. As we'll see, the borders between intuition and other kinds of knowing—unconscious, psychic, subjective, imaginative, mystical—can be quite fluid. Yet, as with mesa and desert or meadow and woods, there are differences which are useful to note if we want to find our own way around and through these experiences with greater consciousness.

The Non-Rational

One whole region where intuition is often placed is the non-rational. Popularly intuition is interpreted as happening when "I knew it was true but I didn't really know why." This usage is supported by the dictionary definition: "the immediate knowing or learning of something without the conscious use of reasoning; instantaneous apprehension" (Webster).

Much of what we know, unconscious projection, psychic forecasts, sensory awareness, mystical vision, we know immediately, without relying on reason. Whether a spirit guide whispers something to us or whether we find out from burning our fingers, there are many things we know without knowing why we know them.

Within the province of the non-rational are traps laid by rationalists to keep it off limits to anyone who considers himself a "reasonable man." Experiences are labeled "irrational" and defined as "lacking the power to reason, senseless, absurd, [implying] mental unsoundness... bad judgement, willfulness" (Webster).

Once we pioneers move beyond these barriers, however, we are free to explore how intuition and various non-rational experiences flank each other. Helping us mark our trail will be my original definition of intuition as realization of wholeness which is simultaneously internal and external.

One reason intuition is often equated with the unconscious and with the psychic is that our realization of wholeness can depend on missing information, hidden clues which emerge from these often repressed or devalued realms. Because these messages, dream images, verbal slips, flashes of imagery, mental telepathies, clairvoyances often give us a missing link, the final puzzle piece, we imbue them with intuitive magic. Many wonderful intuitions actually depend on this kind of information. But these clues in themselves do not provide intuitive wholeness any more than other sources of information, like sense impressions or facts, do.

For example, I once heard a medium tell a surviving family member that her loved one in the world beyond wished her "not to sell Grandmother's diamond brooch." This information, while apparently psychic, was not intuitive. What if you go to a psychic who tells you that your mother was born in the Philippines with a mole on her hip? Since your mother died ten years ago and you have had no previous contact with this psychic, you are amazed. But essentially she hasn't told you anything you didn't already know (except maybe about the mole) or anything that will help you gain intuitive insight into your mother's life or your own. She has given you a fact, however she got it, not insight. Even if she is reading your mind, mirroring it back to you, the insights gained come from your own reflections on these revelations.

Suppose you tell a friend about a run-in with your boss and she points out, gently, that this is the fifth boss you've confronted about that issue. You defend yourself by arguing your side of the issue. Just then your two dogs get into an altercation about who should be leader of the pack. In a flash you see yourself performing a similar routine over and over, and you begin to detect a pattern originating perhaps in a conflict with one of your parents. Her remembrance of a more complete context, working with an intuitive moment provided by canine companions and assisted by your own willingness to step back from yourself, gives you a new insight.

Often people open to psychic information, like people open to any new information, are better positioned for intuitive insight than those with closed minds and fixed ideas. They are more likely to know about any of the pieces that might suddenly fall into place. Really good psychics are also intuitive. They know how to turn the information they receive into insight. Not only does Sister Rosa know your mother died ten years ago, she also can tell you the reason you can't let go of your daughter. She can guess that you haven't finished grieving for your mother because you haven't yet forgiven her. These are people with dual citizenship in the psychic and the intuitive realms.

Another character with dual citizenship is what Jung calls Active Imagination, a pilot who navigates across that misty, watery zone between conscious and unconscious. This pilot is actually an international voyager, who understands how what is conscious for one person be unconscious for another and what is conscious for one culture may be unconscious for another: the symbolic, the numinous, the emotional, the occult. Although equated with intuition and often assisting intuition, the Active Imagination is assigned particularly to this state between conscious and unconscious and is not necessarily interested, as intuition is, in information from every zone. Not all information which comes to Active Imagination is useful for intuitive insight. Some of this intelligence may just let us know how we're really feeling about a current crisis or choice.

Suppose, for example, that a friend has a new partner whom you just can't stand. Your other friends like him quite a bit, which leaves you wondering why everything he does and says totally irks you. You even have a dream about him doing something annoying you can't quite recall. Why should you dream about such a superficial acquaintance? Working with active imagination you may uncover a slight resemblance between the rasp in his voice and the harsh tone of a first grade teacher who once made fun of you in front of the whole class. Over this thin link was conveyed all the humiliation of that forgotten moment. Active imagination has brought something you were not conscious of into consciousness. This may ease your social life, but it doesn't provide you with intuitive insight.

What about imagination itself? Isn't its internal symbolic knowing just another word for intuition? Imagination is the ability to bring images from the senses, from memory and from invention into consciousness, to play with a myriad of possibilities. Imagination is the sky above the ground of intuition. Using our imagination is like watching clouds change shape. But it takes intuition to make an integral whole from one of these shapes, one of these images.

The Imaginative is a collector of odds and ends; some of these items include inventions by her cousin, Fantasy. The Intuitive is an artist who turns one of these items into something meaningful. They are, as you can imagine, the best of friends.

Probably the most valued ambassador to intuition from the realm of the non-rational is the dream image. Already charged with emotional energy, already full of stories, already speaking the language of the symbolic, this messenger is one of the deepest, most reliable sources we have for intuitive insight.

But she is, nonetheless, a citizen of another country. She would lose her power if she resided permanently in the land of intuition. As with the psychic and the unconscious, not everything she has to say is intuitively meaningful. She may just be reporting on the spiciness of dinner the night before.

Of all the visitors from the non-rational world, the one Philip Goldberg finds most promising for immigration is pre-cognition, knowing what's going to happen before it happens. For Jung this is, in fact, where intuition resides: "Intuition tells you whence [something] comes and where it is going" (*MHS*,49).

Here the boundary between psychic and intuitive is quite blurred. This seeing into the past and into the future may come from an ability to experience eternity in an hour, as Blake describes. If so, this foresight, this particular kind of insight, has its source in an intuitive realization of time, the wholeness of any one moment in which past, present and future are merged. Jung's inclusion of both the blossoming of an event and its roots suggests such fullness of expansion. This growth is not just backward and forward but also sideways, into the place of potentiality as well as probability. With such intuitive realization we can know many possibilities, a multitude of "I told you so's." No doubt the Cassandras, prophets and sybils of our world were and are very intuitive.

But the ability to predict the future as if it were linear, beyond our ken, out there past the horizon, is not intuitive; it is psychic. Psychic knowledge is information received as if through extra senses, beyond ordinary sight, hearing, touch. Seeing through walls, across great distances, into the future is the kind of E.S.P. Jung seems to be implying when he says intuition "is a hunch; it is not the product of a voluntary act" (*MHS*, 49).

For me, however, intuition is a voluntary act. It is not just an experience which provides information, it is an event which gives insight. In creation of meaning it moves toward cognition, toward the empire of reason.

Rational

As we move into the sticky field of rationality, the biggest obstacle we confront is our concept of what is meant by reason. This site has been a battleground, even for allies challenging dominant interpretations of reason as instrumental thinking. Jung placed the blame for modern man's [sic] ills at the feet of the "Goddess Reason" (*MHS*, 91), while many feminists, as we have seen, characterize reason as male. Both, however, see reason as a kind of robot fixed in a locked-step march toward progress, with blinders on, driven from cause to effect or from category to category. When we strip the mask of objectivity from this mechanism, we often find reason at the service of greed, egotism, the need to feel superior, to control. Categorizing, polarizing, tunnel vision, linear logic are too often used to support and justify exploitation, hierarchy and racism.

Just as white, male, middle-class has been the norm for human, so neutrality, cause-effect analysis, dualistic thinking and classification have become a norm for what Americans consider rational. Such instrumental thinking, not reason in a fuller sense, is the monolithic pyramidal structure which blocks our path to intuition. Knowing why, for example, may be insignificant, in other cultures, compared to knowing when. For the Chinese, the simultaneity of events can be more meaningful than understanding the reasons they occurred (Von Franz, 227). But whole cultures, whole groups of people have been dismissed as irrational because their mental abilities serve purposes other than this norm.

As Mary Hawkesworth points out, cognition as it manifests within diverse practices can include perception, conceptualization, inference, representation, reflection, imagination, remembrance, conjecture, rationalization, argumentation, justification, contemplation, ratiocination, speculation, meditation, validation and deliberation as well as intuition:

Even a partial listing of the many dimensions of knowing suggests it is a grave error to attempt to reduce this multiplicity to a unitary model (551).

Revolutions of thought occur when we dismantle walls which have been set up between ways of knowing. In the generation of Freud and Jung, rigid class, race and gender hierarchies depended on strict socialization and control of consciousness. As a result the border between conscious and unconscious was besieged by messages from "below." Our generation, constricted by rational analysis, linear logic and instrumental thinking, tends to censor or celebrate messages from "other sides." We need, in fact, to consider descriptions of their thought processes by those who have been excluded by the norm of rationality so we can discover a more inclusive plan for the territory of reason.

Susanne Langer defined reason as "any appreciation of form, any awareness of pattern" (*FAF*, 29). She equated this awareness of unity with intuition:

All cognition of form is intuitive; all relatedness, distinction, congruence, correspondence of forms, contrast and synthesis in a total Gestalt, can be known only by direct insight, which is intuition. And not only form but formal significance is seen intuitively (*FAF*, 378).

One reason intuition has been exiled from the rule of reason is that some schools of thought consider it a perception, awareness from outside self, rather than a conception, thought constructed within the mind. An opposite reason for its dismissal is that some schools of thought consider it entirely too subjective, not subject to proof or even validation. But part of why intuition is a refugee from western dualistic categories of thought is that it is both external and internal simultaneously.

From a woman's point of view, the intuitive process can be compared to the process between conception to birth. Internal understanding is made possible by interaction with an outside energy. Out of the sudden fusion of subject and object which results from this encounter is a unifying of diverse elements which gives birth to a new insight. As this insight grows, it emerges as an image which can expand beyond boundaries of body or person. With this sense of promise, the intuitive refuses to halt at the dividing line between subject and object, between internal and external thought.

What if wholeness itself is a quality of the continuum of energy/matter which informs both consciousness and world? Then subject and object reflect one another, speak to one another, even at times become one another. This idea of correspondences is as old as micro/macrocosm and as contemporary as the theory of superstrings, postulated by physicists Schwartz and Green, which views matter and energy as interchangeable, woven into a single unified field. If such parallels are true, then to understand this wholeness more fully, we need a mode of thinking like intuition which helps us realize these natural processes from the inside, not just through scientific empiricism.

With the respect for unity intuition teaches us, we can still use our reason to draw lines, make distinctions, recognize diversity, without necessarily breaking everything into pieces, ranking the pieces, slicing ourselves apart and cutting some people out. Reason gives us the zones, sets, scales, planes, dimensions, stages, directions, routes, rhythms and paces with which to understand not just the simplicity of a whole but also its complexity.

Beyond Reason?

As soon as we situate intuition as a solid citizen of a newly liberated nation of reason, we notice her gazing at the mountains. Is she perhaps not just rational, in the finest sense of the word, but extra-rational? How, in other words, do we distinguish intuition from mysticism?

An intuitive source for distinctions between intuition and mysticism can be found in the works of the writers I've already discussed:

> I serve as the filament... The energy builds up and builds up in us, always sent back and back, redoubling the impulse every time, until it breaks through and the light is in me, around me, I am the light (LeGuin, 67).

> It would seem that this small crack in the mystery was opened... Afterward whenever I did not eat for long, I could stare at ordinary people and see their light and gold. I could see their dance (Kingston, 33).

I am not able to see. But I do see more and more... There are beings like flames, like fire, like light... It is as if wind had become fire or flames... The blue is only the matrix of the real light (Lessing, 230).

One day when I was sitting quiet and feeling like a motherless child...it came to me: that feeling of being part of everything, not separate at all. I knew that if I cut a tree, my arm would bleed (Walker, 167).

To see things without attachment, from the outside, and to realize their beauty in itself, how strange! And...lightness has come with a kind of transparency, making oneself invisible and things seen through as one walks, how strange (Woolf, 359)!

You are entering all-time now... Soon you'll be in the layer we call "eventual time." You will be able to do this without losing the ability to come back into the part-time you are used to (Grahn, 173).

Most of the criteria for mystical experiences are realized here: unity, numinosity, transcendence of time and space, paradox, tranquility or joy, a heightened sense of reality.

While intuition is simultaneous realization of wholeness which unites the knower and the known, the mystical knower becomes the known. Duality is totally dissolved, at least for that moment. The person having a mystical experience enters into the wholeness, whether she calls it God, the immanent divine, the All-That-Is, the Absolute, Shekhinah, Kali, the Upholder, Sophia, the Void, ultimate reality, Universal Self, the One, the Tao, the Infinite. With mysticism, it seems, one's core melts whereas with intuition, one's edges dissolve.

Intuition is usually solid enough to provide structure for a whole novel. Mysticism can only be a fleeting moment within that novel. Mysticism or enlightenment or *satori* or *samadhi* or beatific vision or *fana* or cosmic consciousness or rapture or nirvana, even in response to our natural world, lifts us out of our ordinary lives. Intuition, more mundane, enables us to enter our experience at a deeper level.

A helpful symbol system for making this distinction between intuition and mysticism is the Hindu chakra system, the seven energy centers in the body, those vortexes where physical, emotional and psychic energies interact within the human body. Intuition is located within the sixth chakra, the Third Eye, while mysticism takes place through the seventh or Crown chakra.

The Third Eye unifies dualities, inner and outer. It can synthesize multiple realities perceived by the two visible eyes. It is probably located in the frontal lobe, corresponding to Paul McClean's Angelic Brain. Through the Crown chakra, imaged by the thousand-petaled lotus, we lose a sense of our individual identities and merge with the universe. This topmost chakra corresponds with a baby's "soft spot" and seems to be the entrance to near-death and out-of-body experiences.

Through the Third Eye, still in our individual consciousness, we view the world and ourselves horizontally, from the center of our own experience. We connect through identification, empathy, synthesis. Through the Crown we are lifted, metaphorically or actually, into a spiritual realm where "every entity in the world [including our selves] is said to interpenetrate every other entity in the world," where in terms of quantum physics, there is a single, giant, universal field, Whitehead's "seamless coat of the universe" (Wilbur, 38).

This imagery corresponds to Ferrucci's distinction between intuition and illumination, Wilbur's distinction between transpersonal experience and unity consciousness, and Grof's distinction between the immanent divine and the transcendent divine. In each case the second of the pair is considered more elevated. Their need for differentiation by level raises the question whether intuition is a lower form of mysticism, its region the foothills of the Absolute peaks. Evelyn Underhill's description of the second stage of mysticism could, in fact, be equated with Ferruci's higher level of intuition, which he calls "superconscious."

Various systems of classification could suggest that in fact there are as many forms of mysticism as there are of intuition or psychic awareness. While philosophers like Stace drew from a multicultural range of mystical experiences for their descriptions, their concern was for what these experiences had in common, the essence of mysticism. A more contemporary concern is to recognize the diversity of mystical experiences from shamanic trance states to kabbalistic visions of community to the revelations of African-American women like Rebecca Jackson.

In this exploration we may discover that some manifestations of mysticism are as rooted in the actual and concrete as intuition is, not tied to an abstract universal or a transcendent reality. Certainly a merge between subject and object occurs through aesthetic experience's tangible integrations, as evidenced by Rumi's raptures, or through scientific inquiry, as evidenced by McClintock's disappearing self.

These systems of classification could also reflect the compulsion of hierarchical thinking to classify every experience as higher or lower than another. The danger for intuition in these hierarchal rankings lies in their appeal to spiritual ambition. Eager to achieve the view from the top, pilgrims could ignore the daily insights which might make their particular lives more meaningful. Who knows if two steps forward is really progress? I recall the Japanese story of the monk who achieved enlightenment, after years of celibacy, by falling in love with a prostitute. As the Tao reminds us:

The bright Way looks dim. The progressive Way looks retrograde. What a muddled mind I have. All men are bright, bright; I alone am dim, dim" (27).

By emphasizing too much the possibility of bliss or union with all that is, we may ignore intuitions of disaster as well as ecstasy, of shadow sides as well as angelic ones, of chaos as well as cosmos. In our human experience, one wise intuitive system, the *I Ching*, counsels that for every expansion there is contraction, for every fullness, emptiness, for every connection, separation, for every birth, death.

I realize that most spiritual disciplines emphasize the harsh conditions which wait on the path to enlightenment: the dark night of the soul, diabolic regions, the desert, the hindrances. I recognize too that mystical experience can open us to greater trust of intuitive insight. As guide for this tour, however, I am concerned that the rush to the mountain top might obscure the realizations we can discover in the caves and canyons of intuition which are closer to where most of us must live.

In one area mysticism might actually need to rely on intuition. One of the qualities of mysticism, according to William James, is its ineffability: "it defies expression" (242). Other accounts refer to it as soundless, wordless, incommunicable. Yet mysticism has been expressed through the symbolic language of great poets, women and men: Mirabai, Blake, Dickenson, Hopkins, Izumi Shikibu, Basho,

Rilke, Herbert, Uvavnuk, Dante, Bibi Hayati, Angela of Foligno, Machado, Whitman, Kabir, Mechthild of Magdeburg.

Hindu chants, Sufi dancing, Chinese painting as well as images like the language of the birds, the music of the spheres, the dance of saints, the alphabet of the universe all express mysticism communications of mystical experience. While some experts on mysticism dismiss voices and visions as hallucinations, these expressions can be seen as attempts to give form to the formless, to harmonize silence. Symbolic transformation of such experience is the only way it can be expressed.

Of all the zones neighboring intuition, mysticism is probably the closest. From Plotinus on, mystics have called their experiences "spiritual intuitions." Many mystics are also psychic and intuitive. Hildegarde of Bingen, for instance, was a visionary, a psychic healer and an intuitive poet and musician, as well as a charismatic leader. Following her mystical experiences of being flooded with pure light, she heard voices and saw images reflected as if in a pool (Flanagan, 194-95). Symbolic language quickly followed illumination.

Ultimately, the difference may be one of focus. If our scope of vision is vast, we may have a mystical experience. If it is more grounded, our experience may be intuitive. As Dewey observes, within the context of every experience there is potentially a sense of an underlying, larger, more inclusive whole:

> There is something mystical associated with the word "intuition" and any experience becomes mystical to the degree in which the sense, the feeling, of the unlimited envelope becomes intense (194).

Now that we've mapped this territory, it may seem that the intuitive person is either a citizen of the world or a woman without a country of her own. Perhaps intuition is not a place but a process, not a destination but the route as traveled. True, the intuitive process can fit in anywhere. It can draw upon any experience, can tap into any other way of knowing. But intuition's condition of exile or alienation in our society is not a desirable state. To find a true home for intuition, we intuitive explorers must settle within.

The map, we know, is not the territory, not even the intuitive map which records a traveler's experience as well as distances, destinations, and directions. To establish a claim for intuition, we must experience intuitive process more deeply. To do this, we center in our personal experience; ground ourselves in our feelings, with empathy for the feelings of others; view our experience from multiple perspectives and in their fullest contexts; follow the process of their unfolding in a natural, organic way; affirm our power in the changes, making our own connections between facets and phases, allowing our own syntheses between disparate elements; discover our own dynamic symbols to describe unique experiences; revise inherited symbols to describe common experience; tell our stories in a transformative way; and share our stories in the contexts of the stories of others.

Only then will intuition be able to come home to herself.

>   Later
>   the doe came wandering back in the twilight.
>   She stepped through the leaves. She hesitated,
>   sniffing the air.
>   Then she knew everything.
>
>   "1945-1985: Poem for the Anniversary"
>   Mary Oliver

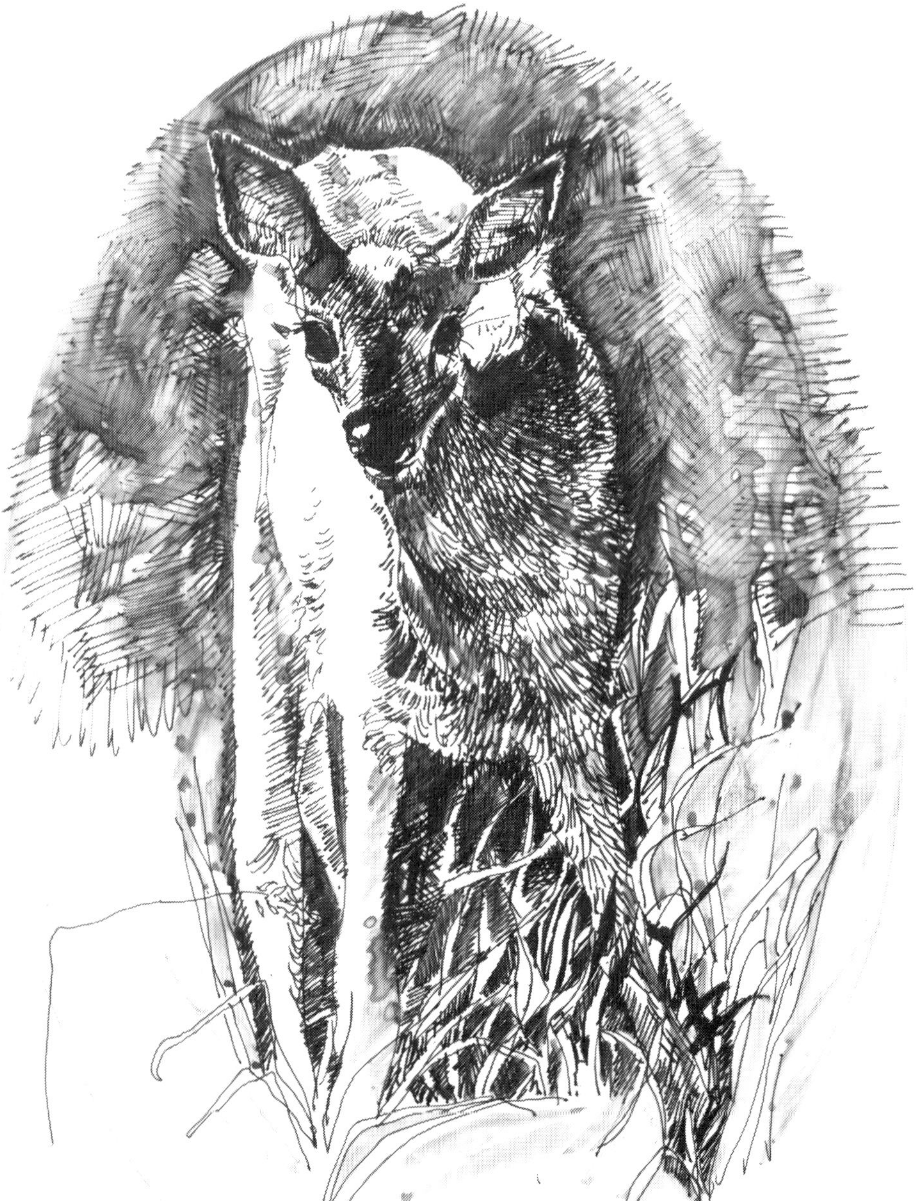

REFERENCES

Amram, Fred Michael. "Invention as Problem-Solving: Special Contributions of Female Inventors." Unpublished paper, 1988.

Assagioli, R. *Psychosynthesis: A Collection of Basic Writings*. New York: Viking, 1965.

Auerback, Nina. "Engorging the Patriarchy." *Feminist Issues in Literary Scholarship*. Edited by Shari Benstock. Bloomington: Indiana University Press, 1987.

Brafford, C.J. and Laine Thom. *Dancing Colors: Paths of Native American Women*. San Francisco: Chronicle Books, 1992.

Bateson, Gregory. *Mind and Nature*. New York: E.P.Dutton, 1979.

Baym, Nina. "The Madwoman and Her Languages: Why I Don't Do Feminist Literary Criticism." *Feminist Issues in Literary Scholarship*. Edited by Shari Benstock. Bloomington: Indiana University Press, 1987.

Belenky, M.F., B.M. Clinchy, N.R. Goldberger and J.M. Tarule. *Women's Ways of Knowing*. New York: Norton, 1987.

Blake, William. *Jerusalem: Selected Poems and Prose*. Edited by Hazard Adams. New York: Holt, Rinehart and Winston, Inc., 1970.

Bleier, Ruth. *Science and Gender: A Critique of Biology and Its Theories on Women*. Pergamon Press, 1984.

Bondurant, Joan. *Conquest of Violence: The Gandhian Philosophy of Conflict*. Berkeley: University of California Press, 1965.

Bowbeer, Anne A. "Sex and the Split Brain: Does the Sex of the Mind Matter?" Unpublished paper, 1988.

Briggs, Katharine C. and Isabel Briggs Myers. *Myers-Briggs Type Indicator*. Palo Alto, California: Consulting Psychologists Press, Inc., 1943, 1976.

Brown, Linda Beatrice. *Rainbow Roun Mah Shoulder*. New York: Ballentine, 1984.

Bruner, Jerome. *On Knowing: Essays for the Left Hand*. Cambridge: Harvard University Press, 1962.

Butler, Octavia. *Kindred*. Boston: Beacon Press, 1979.

Campbell, Joseph. *The Power of Myth*. New York: Doubleday, 1988.

Casey, Joan Frances with Lynn Wilson. *The Flock: The Autobiography of a Multiple Personality*. New York: Alfred A. Knopf, 1991.

Chernin, Kim. *The Flame Bearers*. New York: Harper & Row, 1986.

Chodorow, Nancy. *The Reproduction of Mothering*. Berkeley: University of California Press, 1982.

Cixous, Helene and Catherine Clement. *The Newly Born Woman*. Translated by Betsy Wing. Minneapolis: University of Minnesota Press, 1986 (1975).

Cohan, Clara. *Symbols: The Sacred Language*. Unpublished paper, 1986.

Cohn, Carol. "Sex and Death in the Rational World of Defense Intellectuals." *Signs*. 12:4 (Summer 1987).

Coulter, Dee. *New Paradigms for Understanding the Properties and Functions of the Brain: Implications for Education*. Unpublished paper, 1981.

Davis, Elizabeth. *Women's Intuition*. Berkeley: Celestial Arts, 1989.

Desimone, Diane and Jo Durden-Smith. *Sex and the Brain*. New York: Arbor House, 1983.

Dewey, John. *Art As Experience*. New York: Capricorn, 1958.

Dickenson, Emily. *The Complete Poems*. Edited by Thomas H. Johnson. Boston: Little, Brown and Company, 1960.

Duplessis, Rachel Blau. *Writing Beyond the Ending: Narrative Strategies of Twentieth Century Women Writers*. Bloomington: Indiana University Press, 1985.

Einstein, Albert. *Out of My Later Years*. Secaucus, New Jersey: The Citadel Press, 1956.

Eisler, Riane. *The Chalice and the Blade*. San Francisco: Harper & Row, 1987.

Fausto-Sterling, Anne. *Myths of Gender: Biological Theories About Women and Men*. New York: Basic Books, 1985.

Ferrucci, Piero. *What We May Be*. New York: Tarcher, 1982.

Flanagan, Sabina. *Hildegarde of Bingen*. London: Routledge, 1989.

Forman, Frieda Johles and Caoran Sowton. *Taking Our Time: Feminist Perspectives on Temporality*. New York: Pergamon Press, 1989.

Fyre, Joanne S. *Living Stories, Telling Lives*. Ann Arbor: The University of Michigan Press, 1986.

Gardner, Howard. *Frames of Mind: The Theory of Multiple Intelligences.* New York: Basic Books, 1983.

Gardner, Joy. *Color and Crystals: A Journey Through the Chakras.* Freedom, CA: Crossing Press, 1988.

Gimbutas, Marija. *The Language of the Goddess.* San Francisco: Harper and Row, 1989.

Goldberg, Philip. *The Intuitive Edge.* New York: Tarcher, 1985.

Gonzales-Wippler, M. *A Kabbalah for the Modern World.* New York: Bantam, 1974.

Gould, June. *The Writer in All of Us.* New York: New American Library, 1989.

Graham, F. Lanier, Ed. *The Rainbow Book.* Berkeley: Shambhala, 1975.

Grahn, Judy. *The Work of a Common Woman.* Oakland, Ca.: Diana Press, 1978.

_____ *Mundane's World.* Freedom, Ca.: The Crossing Press, 1988.

Greenbie, Barrie. "'Speaking with Names': Language and Landscape Among the Western Apache," *Cultural Anthropology* 3 (2): 99-130, 1988.

Greene, Gayle and Coppelia Kahn, eds. *Making a Difference: Feminist Literary Criticism.* London and New York: Methuen, 1985.

Grima, Benedicte. *The Performance of Emotion Among Paxtun Women.* Austin: University of Texas Press, 1992.

Grof, Stanislav, Ed. "Spirituality, Alcoholism and Drug Abuse," *ReVision, A Journal of Consciousness and Change,* 10:2.

_____ *Beyond the Brain: Death, Birth, and Transcendence in Psychotherapy.* Albany: SUNY Press, 1985.

Gruber, Howard, Glenn Terrell, Michael Wertheimer, eds. *Contemporary Approaches to Creative Thinking.* New York: Atherton Press, 1962.

Harding, Sandra and Hintikka, M.B., eds. *Discovering Reality: Feminist Perspectives on Epistemology, Metaphysics, Methodology, and Philosophy of Science.* Dordrecht, Holland: Reidel, 1983.

Hawkesworth, Mary E. "Knowers, Knowing, Known: Feminist Theory and Claims of Truth." *Signs* 14:3, (1989).

Heilbrun, Carolyn. *Writing A Woman's Life.* New York: Norton, 1988.

Hopkins, Gerard Manley. *Poems and Prose of Gerard Manley Hopkins*. Baltimore: Penquin Books, 1953.

Hwong, Lucia. *House of Sleeping Beauties*. [A Music Tape.] New York: Private Music, 1985.

James, William. *The Essential Writings*. Edited by Bruce Wilshire. Albany: SUNY Press, 1984.

Joyce, James. *The Portable James Joyce*. Edited by Harry Levin. New York: The Viking Press, 1947.

Jung, Carl, and M.L. von Franz, Joseph L. Henderson, Jolande Jacobi, Aniela Jaffe. *Man and His Symbols*. New York: Dell, 1968.

Jung, Carl G. *The Portable Jung*. New York: Viking Penguin, 1971.

_____ *Analytical Psychology: Its Theory and Practice*. New York: Vintage Books, 1968.

Kabir. *The Kabir Book*. Translated by Robert Bly. Boston: Beacon Press, 1977.

Keller, Evelyn Fox. A *Feeling for the Organism: The Life and Work of Barbara McClintock*. New York: W.H. Freeman, 1983.

Kingston, Maxine Hong. *The Woman Warrior*. New York: Random House, 1975.

Kristeva, Julia. "Women's Time." *Signs* 7:1 (Autumn, 1981).

Kroeber, Theodora. *Ishi: The Last of His Tribe*. New York: Bantam, 1964.

Kyselka, Will. *An Ocean in Mind*. Honolulu: University of Hawaii Press, 1987.

Langer, Susanne. *Feeling and Form*. New York: Scribner's, 1953.

_____ *Philosophy in a New Key*. New York: New American Library, 1962.

_____ *Mind: An Essay on Human Feeling*. Baltimore: Johns Hopkins University Press, 1988.

Lawrence, W. Gordon. "Won from the void and formless infinite: experiences of social dreaming." *Free Associations* (1991) Volume 2, Part 2 (No. 22), 259-294.

LeGuin, Ursula. *Dancing at the Edge of the World*. New York: Grove, 1989.

_____ *The Left Hand of Darkness*. New York: The Berkeley Publishing Group, 1969.

_____ "Up To Earth": *A Review of Mundane's World. Women's Review of Books* (Fall, 1988).

Lerner, Gerda. *The Creation of Feminist Consciousness*. New York: Oxford University Press, 1993.

LeSueur, Meridel. "Harvest." *Ripening: Selected Work 1927-1980*. Edited by Elaine Hedges. Old Westbury, New York: Feminist Press, 1982.

Lessing, Doris. *The Marriage Between Zones Three, Four, and Five*. New York: Random House, 1981.

Levi-Strauss, Claude. *The Savage Mind*. Chicago: The University of Chicago Press, 1962.

Lippard, Lucy. *Overlay: Contemporary Art and the Art of Prehistory*. New York: Pantheon, 1983.

Lutz, Catherine and Lila Abu-Lughod. *Language and the Politics of Emotion*. Cambridge: Cambridge University Press, 1990.

Meeker, Joseph. *The Comedy of Survival*. New York: Scribner, 1974.

Merriam, Eve. "Maria Mitchell, Astronomer." *Growing Up Female in America: Ten Lives*. Garden City, N.Y.: Doubleday, 1971.

Metzner, Ralph. *Maps of Consciousness*. New York: Collier, 1971.

Miller, Jean Baker. *Toward A New Psychology of Women*. Boston: Beacon, 1976.

Minnich, Elizabeth. "Translation: The Eternal Mystery of Change." Unpublished paper, 1988.

_____ *Transforming Knowledge*. Philadelphia: Temple University Press, 1990.

Mitchell, Stephen. *The Enlighened Heart*. New York: Harper & Row, 1989.

Mahony, William K. "The Artist as Yogi, the Yogi as Artist." *Parabola* 8:1 (Spring, 1988).

Monaghan, Patricia. *Sun Goddesses*. Unpublished manuscript, 1988.

Moore, Thomas, ed. *Blue Fire: Selected Writings by James Hillman*. New York: Harper Perennial, 1989.

Moulton, Janice. "A Paradigm of Philosophy: The Aversary Method." *Discovering Reality*. Edited by Sandra Harding and Merrill Hintikka. Boston: D. Reidel Publishing Company, 1983.

Needleman, Jacob, ed. *The Sword of Gnosis*. Baltimore: Penquin Books, 1974.

Ni, Hua-Ching. Tao. *Los Angeles: The Shrine of the Eternal Breath of Tao*, 1979.

Noble, Vicki. *Motherpeace*. San Francisco: Harper and Row, 1983.

Noel, Daniel. *Approaching Earth*. Amity, New York: Amity House, 1986.

O'Brien, Mary. *The Politics of Reproduction*. Boston: Routledge & Kegan Paul, 1981.

O'Keeffe, Georgia. *Georgia O'Keeffe*. New York: Viking, 1976.

Oliver, Mary. *Dream Work*. New York: The Atlantic Monthly Press, 1986.

Oliveros, Pauline. "Sonic Meditations." *Scores: An Anthology of New Music*. New York: Smith Publications, 1974.

Olsen, Tillie. *Silences*. Lawrence: Delaconte Press, 1978.

Ong, Walter J. *The Barbarian Within*. New York: The MacMillan Company, 1962.

Ostriker, Alice. "The Thieves of Language." *Signs*, 8:1.

The Oxford English Dictionary. Oxford University Press, 1933.

Peay, Pythia. "The Singing Sword: Images Guide Adolescents' Journeys." *Common Boundary*, 8:1 (February, 1990).

Perera, Sylvia Brinton. *Descent to the Goddess: A Way of Initiation for Women*. Toronto: Inner City Books, 1981.

Pierce, Joseph Chilton. *The Magical Child*. N.Y.: Bantam, 1977.

_____ *The Magical Child Matures*. N.Y.: Dutton,1985.

Piercy, Marge. *To Be of Use*. Garden City, New York: Doubleday & Company, 1969.

Psychic Powers. Alexandria, Va.: Time-Life Books, 1989.

Reis, Patricia. "Facing Medusa: The Dark Goddess and Creativity." *Insight*, 4:3 (1985).

Rich, Adrienne. *The Dream of a Common Language*. New York: W.W. Norton & Company, Inc., 1978.

Rilke, Rainer Maria. *Letters*. Translated by Jane Bannard Greene and M.D. Herter. New York: W.W. Norton, 1948.

Rodegast, Pat and Judith Stanton. *Emmanuel's Book*. New York: Bantam, 1985.

Roget's International Thesaurus (Third Edition). New York: Thomas Y. Crowell Company, 1962.

Rosen, Stanley. *Plato's Symposium*. New Haven: Yale University Press, 1968.

Samuels, Mike and Nancy Samuels. *Seeing with the Mind's Eye*. New York: Random House, 1975.

Scholem, Gershom. *Kabbalah*. New York: Dorset Press, 1974.

Shah, Idries. *Tales of the Dervishes*. New York: E.P. Dutton, 1967.

Showalter, Elaine. "Women's Space and Time." *Feminist Issues in Literary Scholarship*. Edited by Shari Benstock. Bloomington: Indiana University Press, 1987.

Stace, Walter. *The Teachings of the Mystics*. New York: New American Library, 1960.

Starhawk. *The Spiral Dance*. San Francisco: Harper & Row, 1979.

Stone, Merlin. *Ancient Mirrors of Womanhood*. New York: New Sibylline Books, 1979.

Thompson, Robert Farris. *Flash of the Spirit*. New York: Vintage, 1983.

Tzu, Lao. *Tao Teh Ching*. Translated by Dr. John C.H. Wu. New York: St. John's University Press, 1961.

Torre, Susanna, ed. *Women in Architecture: A Historic and Contemporary Perspective*. New York: The Whitney Library of Design, 1977.

Underhill, Evelyn. *The Essentials of Mysticism*. New York: E.P. Dutton, 1960.

V., Rachel. *Family Secrets: Life Stories of Adult Children of Alcoholics*. San Francisco: Harper & Row, 1987.

Vaughn, Frances. *Awakening Intuition*. Garden City, New York: Doubleday Anchor, 1979.

Walker, Alice. *The Color Purple*. New York: Harcourt Brace Jovanovich, 1982.

Walker, Barbara G., Ed. *The Women's Encyclopedia of Myths and Secrets*. San Francisco: Harper and Row, 1983.

Watts, Alan W. *Psychotherapy East and West*. New York: Random House, 1961.

Webster's New World Dictionary of the American Language. New York: The World Publishing Company, 1962.

Whitehead, Alfred North. *Modes of Thought*. New York: The MacMillan Company, 1938.

Whitehill, Sharon. "Voices from the Night: Keeping a Dream Diary." *Women's Diaries*, 3:3. Edited by Jane DuPree Begos. (Fall, 1985).

Whitman, Walt. *Whitman*. Edited by Leslie Fiedler. New York: Dell Publishing Co., 1959.

Wickes, Frances. *The Inner World of Childhood*. New York: Appleton-Century, 1927, 1966.

Wilbur, Ken. *No Boundaries*. Boulder: Shambhala, 1981.

Wilhelm, Richard, translator. (Cary F. Barnes, English translator). *The I Ching*. Princeton: Princeton University Press, 1950.

Willis, Susan. "Black Women Writers: Taking A Critical Perspective." *Making a Difference: Feminist Literary Criticism*. Edited by Gayle Greene and Coppelia Kahn. New York: Methuen, 1985.

Woolf, Virginia. *A Writer's Diary*. London: Hogarth, 1965.

_____ *The Waves*. New York: Harcourt, Brace, 1931.

Woodman, Marion. *Addiction to Perfection*. Toronto: Inner City Books, 1982.

Zimmerman, Bonnie. "What Has Never Been: An Overview of Lesbian Feminist Criticism." *Making a Difference: Feminist Literary Criticism*. Edited by Gayle Greene and Coppelia Kahn. New York: Methuen, 1985.

INDEX

A

Aborigines 32, 35, 163
abortion 4, 66, 111-113, 129, 160, 163
abuse 21, 57, 91, 104, 113, 128, 129, 143, 147, 161-165, 171, 184
action 3, 6
Active Imagination 31, 190
African 22, 35, 50, 51, 54, 97, 169
African-American 51, 54, 115, 146-148, 158, 169, 187, 196
American 19, 20, 26, 50, 51, 54, 99, 100, 115, 145, 148, 168, 169, 172
analogy 33, 101, 169, 172
animals 22, 51, 88, 94, 99, 103, 126, 140, 161, 171
anthropology 120
anti-Semitism 55
Apache 25, 26, 32, 35
apartheid 171
archetype 71, 90, 91, 110, 146
art 2, 13, 24, 25, 35, 44, 50, 58, 74, 112, 130, 144, 161-165, 168

B

Blake, William 1, 13
body 3, 9, 17, 20, 21, 28, 40, 41, 49, 64, 92, 101, 117, 130, 152, 166, 168, 193, 196
brain 11, 13, 31-36, 44, 77, 167, 179, 180, 187, 196
Buddha 1
Buddhism 27

C

chakras 71, 91, 101, 105, 140, 155
change 6, 12, 15, 22, 37, 50, 58, 72, 79, 88, 104-106, 114, 143, 145, 150-154, 158
children 4, 18, 51, 57, 70-76, 79, 88, 89, 100, 127, 155, 161, 167, 170, 171, 183-184
Chinese 32, 35, 53, 54, 97-101, 129, 169, 192, 198
classism 146
cognition 11, 38, 179, 192, 193
color 27, 28, 60, 111, 136, 146, 183
community 2-5, 7, 10, 12, 24, 48, 94, 107, 128, 130, 134, 143, 146-149, 150, 154, 158, 162, 170, 196
compassion 20, 44, 57, 103, 128
conception 35, 41, 112, 120, 193
creativity 2, 5, 15, 37, 68, 107, 108, 112, 120, 122, 136, 137, 141, 165, 170

D

deer 1, 49, 55, 132, 187
Dewey, John 10, 33, 41-44, 163, 183, 186, 188, 198
dichotomy 180
Dickenson, Emily 32, 44, 177, 197
diversity 3, 50, 51, 58, 107, 110, 128, 145, 153, 161, 164, 168-171, 180, 194, 196
divisions 57, 170
drama 28, 73, 86, 140, 168
dreams 22, 29, 43, 58, 65, 76, 79, 109-112, 163
drug abuse 4, 129, 165

E

education 4, 6, 14, 37, 53, 109, 118, 122, 129, 160-171, 177
Einstein 30, 31, 41, 44
either/or 106, 161, 180
emotion 13, 27, 60, 66, 74, 103, 107, 110, 114-117, 128, 143, 144, 164, 165, 181-184
empathy 14, 18, 19, 20, 34, 38, 66, 110-113, 116, 123, 139, 186, 196, 199
energy 1, 5, 10-14, 17, 19-21, 23, 27, 39, 40, 52, 62, 68, 75, 79, 83, 90-94, 101-103, 112, 138, 139, 153, 155, 191-194
environment 3, 21, 24, 50, 78, 86, 121, 171
ethnic cleansing 127, 171
ethnicity 57, 107, 145, 177
experience 1, 4, 5, 10-14, 17
expertise 129, 160

expressive arts therapies 2, 166

F

failure 61, 126, 128, 139, 140, 153, 185
Fausto-Sterling, Anne 11, 179
feminism 2, 3, 11, 16, 18, 24, 37, 56, 57, 90, 92, 96, 108, 140, 145, 154, 157, 171, 179, 180, 185, 192
Ferrucci, Piero 10, 13, 41-43
Forster, E.M. 126
friendship 40, 96

G

Gandhi 126, 127
genius 2, 11, 12, 34-36
gods 90, 146, 148, 149, 162, 195
goddesses 75, 90, 110, 114, 146, 155, 192
Goldberg, Philip 178, 179, 191
Grahn, Judy 128, 145, 155, 157, 158, 195
Grail 56, 170

H

Hawaiian 35
hearing 25, 33, 62, 96, 192
Hebrew 32
hemispheres of the brain 11, 179
hierarchy 36, 56, 57, 94, 103, 146, 180, 192,
Hildegarde of Bingen 177, 198
history 89, 128, 156, 161, 172
holocaust 171
homophobia 94, 146
Hopi 108
house 4, 28, 51, 79, 128, 130-135, 139-144, 147, 157, 181

I

I Ching 92, 110, 197
identification 14, 18-20, 40, 41, 79, 99, 110, 118, 119, 123, 177, 186, 196
illiteracy 4, 129, 167

image 4, 5, 10, 13, 14, 17, 22, 24, 27-29, 32-36, 39, 40, 42, 60, 62, 71, 72, 90, 110, 111, 146, 147, 150, 153, 169, 172, 191, 193
imagination 16, 25, 26, 31, 40, 48, 65, 75, 78, 86, 110, 130, 165-167, 190-192
indigenous people 35
insight 1, 2, 6, 10-12, 18-22, 31, 34, 37-40, 48, 66, 73, 101, 106, 115, 117, 120, 126, 144, 149, 156, 157, 160, 165, 171, 184, 185, 189-193
instinct 176
instrumental thinking 31, 192, 193
integration 5, 11, 17, 75, 94, 97, 107, 111-115, 139, 163, 179
intuition (see table of contents for specific discussions on intuition)
Iroquois 33, 127

J

James, William 24, 165, 197
Joyce, James 13
Jung 10, 17, 23, 90, 165, 182, 183, 190-193

K

Kingston, Maxine Hong 14, 70, 91, 92, 101, 104, 105, 194

L

Langer, Susanne 10, 13, 21, 35, 41, 43, 147, 148, 185, 193, 119
language 1, 2, 7, 12, 13, 22, 24, 32, 35, 50, 51, 58, 70-72, 89-91, 96, 106-109, 114-117, 129, 145, 163, 167-173, 191, 197, 198
learning styles 168
LeGuin, Ursula 14, 31, 70, 91-93, 96, 101-105, 159, 180, 194
Lerner, Gerda 177
lesbian 54, 146, 154, 158, 187
literature 4, 6

M

MacLean, Paul 34
McClintock, Barbara 18, 42, 118-120, 185
merger 19, 185
metaphor 13, 24, 34, 36, 40, 43, 97, 172
Minnich, Elizabeth 19, 42, 172
morality 128
multicultural 3, 129, 168-170, 196
multiple personality disorder 19
multiplicity 3, 4, 7, 14, 24, 54, 56, 108, 150, 154, 193
music 22, 29, 33, 49, 61, 74, 75, 108, 110-112, 168, 198
mysticism 24, 31, 102, 194-197
myth 2, 14, 23, 66, 88, 111, 148, 162

N

Native American 56, 140, 169
nature 6, 13, 22, 38, 42, 44, 58, 65, 78, 88, 126, 139, 153, 171, 173, 180, 183
non-traditional education 170, 171

O

Oliver, Mary 199

P

paradox 14, 22, 27, 195
patriarchy 180, 105, 106
Paxtun 184
perception 5, 6, 11, 21, 31, 39, 88, 97, 140, 154, 168, 179, 186, 192, 193
Perera, Sylvia 19, 43, 185
perfection 64, 140, 159
philosophy 1, 4, 41, 127, 160
playacting 72-76, 86, 88
poetry 44, 68, 113, 172, 187
politics 87, 110, 170, 181
pollution 183
poverty 52, 54, 183, 187
psychic knowledge 191
psychology 2, 4, 6-7, 36, 108, 110

R

racism 10, 35, 56, 57, 91, 129, 146, 148, 192
rainbow 75, 79, 90, 110, 145, 146, 155
reason 20, 32, 34, 41, 180, 189, 192-94
recovery 2, 166
Rich, Adrienne 7
ritual 111, 132, 140, 168, 169

S

science 23, 24, 41, 78, 87, 120, 172
Senoi 163
sensation 27, 32, 128, 131, 144
sexual preference 57, 107, 145, 177
snake 75, 90, 149, 155
spiral 64, 90, 110, 112, 133, 154-156, 183
storytelling 23, 74, 75, 87
Sufi 30, 169, 198
symbol 1, 10, 15, 22, 32, 33, 41, 55, 75, 88, 90-93, 97, 101, 108, 130, 145, 146, 154, 155, 168, 172, 185, 195
synthesis 2, 5, 6, 10, 17, 23, 40, 104, 107, 111, 112, 139, 163, 164, 168, 193, 196
systems theory 126

T

talent 35, 112, 137
tao 33, 92, 94, 99, 169, 195, 197
therapy 6, 37, 114, 184
thinking 3, 26, 31, 38, 57, 62, 65, 88, 101, 121, 128, 131, 143-145, 160, 164, 170, 180, 187, 192-194, 197
Thompson, Robert Farris 22
time 13, 23, 32, 33, 59, 62, 64, 78, 86, 94, 105, 110, 143, 144, 157, 181-183, 186, 191, 194, 195
tone 28, 33, 147, 158, 168, 190

transformation 5, 17, 23, 58, 75, 94, 96, 100, 104-107, 111, 134, 144, 146, 148, 154-157, 163, 172, 184, 198
Truth, Sojourner 126, 177

U

unity 23, 51, 92, 96, 104, 141, 145, 150-154, 169, 182, 193-196

V

Vaughn, Frances 19, 41, 43, 178, 186, 120
vision 5, 22-24, 27, 33, 58, 61, 74, 90, 92, 97, 109, 113-115, 126, 130, 136, 139, 144, 148, 149, 153, 156, 157, 169, 171, 182, 183, 189, 192, 195, 198
voice 1, 17, 28, 59, 62, 64, 96, 97, 100, 101, 105, 114, 117, 153, 154, 163, 168, 176, 178, 190
void 92, 106, 152, 195, 204
Von Franz, Marie-Louise 23, 42, 192

W

Walker, Alice 128, 145-149, 158, 195
war 19, 28, 54, 55, 57, 94, 126, 127, 184, 187
ways of knowing 10, 12, 31, 109, 120, 171, 193
wheel of fortune 110, 145-148
Whitman, Walt 198
wholeness 1, 4-6, 10, 12, 21-23, 31, 33, 53, 56, 58, 92-96, 99, 104, 105, 127, 130, 131-135, 139, 141, 143, 146, 189, 191, 194, 195
Wilbur, Ken 17, 27, 196
women 4, 7, 10-13, 35-37, 53, 56, 57, 60, 62, 66-71, 91, 94, 98, 100, 101, 104-106, 111, 118-121, 127, 130, 135, 145, 154, 157-161, 171, 172, 177-187, 197

women's movement 2, 7, 24, 38, 56, 96, 157, 162
women's studies 60, 70, 71, 107, 108, 116, 160, 162, 172
Women's Ways of Knowing 37, 38, 108, 109
Woodman, Marion 159, 180
Woolf, Virginia 15, 16, 33, 128, 145, 149, 150-154, 158, 195
worship 126, 149, 151

Y

yin/yang 71, 90-93, 96-99, 104-106, 110, 155, 183

Margaret Blanchard

A writer and poet, Margaret Blanchard's poetry is included in *Unlacing: Ten Irish-American Poets*. For twenty-five years she lived in Baltimore where she was an editor for *Women: A Journal of Liberation*, served on the staff of The Women's Growth Center and taught women's studies and writing at Towson State University. Her Ph.D. in literature and women's studies is from The Union Institute. Now as core faculty for the Graduate Program of Vermont College, she serves students in the Mid-Atlantic and upstate New York. She lives with human, canine and feline friends in a house some of them built together in the Adirondacks. She also does photography and stained glass art.